Outlaws of the Black Hills and Wyoming

By Doug Engebretson

Library of Congress No. 82-62073
ISBN No. 0-913062-36-7
Copyright © 1982
All Rights Reserved

Published by:
Dakota West Books
Dave Strain
Rapid City, SD 57701
www.dakotawestbooks.com

Printed by:
Fenske Media Corp
Rapid City, SD 57703
Printed in U.S.A.

1st Edition: 1982
2nd Edition: 2006

Empty Saddles, Forgotton Names

Outlaws of the Black Hills and Wyoming

by Doug Engebretson

DEDICATION

To Pat, who made it all possible.

PREFACE

The Old West has fascinated Americans for generations. A place where social controls were obscured and the land unexploited and unspoiled, it appeals to a spirit of adventure. Especially, the outlaws of the Old West fascinate the public. Drifting beyond the pale of acceptable behavior, they intrigue and beguile those who hold their impulses in control. Who can conceal an interest in Jesse James or Billy the Kid?

The high degree of popularity in outlaws of the Old West is visible in the numerous publications about them. To page through the annotated titles compiled by Ramon F. Adams in his **Six-Guns and Saddle Leather: A Bibliography of Books and Pamphlets on Western Outlaws and Gunmen** is an exhausting experience as it enumerates hundreds of publications. Even specializing on one figure, Billy the Kid, allowed Jeff Dykes to compile a book-length bibliography. Recent books about outlaws continue to appear and to single one out as an example of the continuing fascination is dangerous; however, the **Encyclopedia of Western Gun-Fighters** by Bill O'Neal, which compiles brief biographies and commentary on "every outlaw deserving attention," certainly warrants comment.

Doug Engebretson's work on the outlaws of the Black Hills and Wyoming joins this list of new publications and fills a significant void in the topic. While the Black Hills region has generated many studies, enumerated nicely in J. Leonard Jennewein's **Black Hills Booktrails**, little has been done to systematically examine the bandits. They are lightly studied in several popular books in which an outlaw occasionally becomes the subject of a chapter or colorful narrative, but no extensive study comes to mind. General books about outlaws give brief attention to the Black Hills and Wyoming region, mentioning only well-known figures and neglecting many more important because their flamboyant reputations were not made famous by the Dime Novels.

There are several prerequisites for a good book on outlaws. One, which has predominated, is to present the story in a colorful manner. While clarity and interest are important, a criteria which I regard more valuable is accuracy. There are many books which present colorful narratives concerning some Black Hills outlaws, but too often they are inaccurate and based upon legend or hearsay. The colorful reputations of outlaws caused many a good story to appear in print and unfortunately too many authors do not check the origin or accuracy of the stories. Fortunately, Doug has done his research and his notes detail the inaccuracies in Black Hills literature. He has compared and cross-examined accounts, checked the sparse original sources, and used common sense to make decisions regarding the veracity of the stories. Visit Doug and he will overwhelm you with the detailed mistakes he has uncovered in the published materials which repeat earlier errors and add new ones. Doug is an enthusiast for his subject and for the truth.

Doug has written a short narrative about selected outlaws and robberies in the Black Hills and Wyoming region. The book is in the style of an anthology or collection rather than a narrative history of banditry in the region. It is unfortunate that Doug, for purposes of space, had to delete several of his chapters; they will, undoubtedly, appear in different locations as articles during the next few years. This book, however, compiles significant new material about selected outlaws of the Black Hills and Wyoming region. It is an interesting selection including both some well-known and some previously neglected figures. Included are the stories of Lame Johnny, Robert "Reddie" McKimie, Jim McCloud, the George Axelby gang, Dunc Blackburn, and Big Nose George.

It is refreshing to read accounts which extensively utilize early newspapers and accounts and to know the author is sincerely attempting to decipher the truth so often desired and so seldom found in Western history. Doug's book should find its way into regional libraries and collections both for reference and general interest. The appeal of Black Hills outlaws and gunslingers is seen each summer in the reenactment of the trial of Jack McCall and in the visitations by tourists to the graves of Wild Bill Hickok and Calamity Jane at Mount Moriah. Certainly this book on outlaws of the Black Hills and Wyoming should strike a chord with people who want to pursue the outlaws beyond the veneer of popularity and learn what they were really like and what they were really about.

James McLaird
Dakota Wesleyan University
Mitchell, South Dakota

TABLE OF CONTENTS

THE CANYON SPRINGS ROBBERY

The evening of September 25, 1878, messenger Eugene Smith was heard to say: "You'll notice that while those fellows hold up stages and rob the passengers every day or two, they haven't tackled the treasure coach. The boys would find that a different kind of nut to crack, and we would like to have them try it."[1] The new treasure coach, the Iron Clad, nicknamed the Moniter, inspired that kind of confidence. Built by the A. D. Butler & Co. of Cheyenne, the Iron Clad was lined with five-sixteenths inch steel plate. Two port holes, cut in the doors, promised to give the messengers inside "the dead wood on any and all road agents." Inside was the safe that had "carried so much treasure out of the Black Hills for the past six months." The safe was supposed to be able to withstand efforts to open it for twenty-four hours. Heavy rifles had been fired into the sides of the treasure coach from a distance of fifty feet "without the least effect."[2]

Until mid-May, 1878, when the Iron Side was added to the line, regular Concord coaches, heavily guarded by shotgun messengers and equipped with special safes, doubled as treasure coaches. The local press, with reports of the amount of treasure taken out, gave the management of the stage company a justifiable uneasiness: "The treasure coach which arrived yesterday, brought in thirty-one thousand dollars worth of Black Hills gold," reported the **Cheyenne Daily Leader** in April.[3] The reports were routinely made. While such notices served to disprove doubters like Leander P. Richardson who, in 1876, wrote: "I have no hesitation in saying that I think the Black Hills will eventually prove a failure,"[4] they were a direct challenge to the road agents to "tackle" the treasure coach. (That remark, incidentally, earned Richardson the nickname "Puttyhead" around Cheyenne.)

Despite the reports of the huge sums of treasure carried out of the Black Hills by the treasure coach, it travelled unchallenged by the road agents. The Moniter arrived in Deadwood from Cheyenne for its regularly scheduled trip on September 25, 1878. On the way up messengers Jesse Brown, Boone May, and Billy Sample were let off at Beaver Station. They would pick up the treasure coach there, and guard it through to Hat Creek by horseback on the down trip. Messengers Gale Hill, Gene Smith, and Scott Davis continued into Deadwood with the Moniter.[5] The next morning, September 26, 1878, the Moniter rolled out of Deadwood with Gene Barnett at the reins. Messenger Gale Hill, "one of the pluckiest men who ever struck the West," rode the boot by his side. Inside were messengers Scott Davis and "we would like to have them try it" Smith. Although passengers were expressly forbidden from riding on the Moniter Hugh O. Campbell, a telegraph operator on his way to Jenny's Stockade, was also inside by special permission.[6] Division Superintendent William Ward accompanied the coach on horseback. Ward, instructed by Luke Voorhees to accompany the coach as far as Hat Creek, turned around before they arrived at Canyon Springs, a relay station about thirty-five miles out of Deadwood.[7]

Hours after the Moniter left Deadwood the entire Black Hills region was aghast at the news that the Moniter had been robbed at Canyon Springs. Hugh Campbell was dead; Gale Hill was thought to be dying; Gene Smith, wounded; and the safe, guaranteed unopenable for twenty-four hours, had been cracked in three or four hours.

William Miner, the stock tender at Canyon Springs, later told Voorhees how the robbers secured their position for the attack and accomplished the impossible with relative ease:

> Shortly before time for the stage to arrive from Deadwood, a man on horseback rode up and asked for a drink of water. Upon dismounting, he ordered me to throw up my hands, which I did. He then pushed me in the grain room of the stable. By this time the band of five, I thought there were six of them, all got in the stable and proceeded to make arrangements for the capture of the coach.
> They removed the mud or chinking from between the logs near the door of the stable, where the stage always stops . . .[8]

Gale Hill jumped down off the coach when the Moniter came to a stop and walked to the back of the coach to place a block of wood behind the wheels. That done, Hill started for the barn and the robbers "opened fire without calling any holdup or saying a word." Hill was shot through the body and was wounded again as he raised his gun to fire at his attackers.[9] Campbell was severely wounded in the head,[10] and the ball passed through him and struck Smith, "knocking him senseless." Smith slumped to the floor of the coach — where he remained until the fight was over. Said Davis, "We supposed he was dead."[11] Davis told Campbell that he was going to get out of the coach and behind a large pine tree across the road. Campbell said that if Davis was going, so was he. Davis, with the coach between himself and the robbers, began backing his way across the road "shooting at anything and everything that looked like a robber."[12] Davis said about half way across Campbell veered to the left and was hit, then fatally shot. Davis said:

Just before I reached the tree, one of the robbers showed up and exposed himself, at the head of the team, as I was urging the stage driver to make a run for it and get out of there. Just as this robber exposed himself, I turned and quickly fired, wounding him badly. He threw up his hands, fell over backwards, crawled behind the horses and made his getaway to the back of the barn . . .[13]

Hill had rallied and crawled into the barn. Hill fired from the window and wounded another of the robbers, later identified as Frank McBride, then fainted from the loss of blood.[14]

Galen "Gale" Hill. *(Photo: Courtesy Wyoming State Archives, Museums, and Historical Department.)*

Barnett failed to heed Davis' pleadings and was captured by Charles Carey, the leader of the outlaws. Carey pushed Barnett to the back of the coach and placed Barnett directly in front of him. He then advanced toward Davis' position behind the tree. Davis, seeing that he could not fire at the advancing robber without hitting Barnett, said he remembered Luke Voorhees had told him the safe was guaranteed for twenty-four hours and backed through the pine trees to summon help. According to William Miner, after Davis left "the band rounded up all the men about the place and tied them to the trees, saying that at ten o'clock a man would be along to release them."[15] Miner said that the robbers "immediately" went to work on the safe, but the **Black Hills Journal** reported:

> . . . The robbers then went to work at the coach, running it in the timber, and succeeded in getting out the heavy iron treasure box, breaking it open and secure the treasure, consisting of gold bullion valued at $27,000, beside jewelry and a small amount of currency.[16]

According to Miner opening the safe that was guaranteed for twenty-four hours only required "several hours of work." He said he was released at "half past nine or ten o'clock," and immediately started for Deadwood.[17]

One of the treasure boxes that was used on the Cheyenne-Deadwood route. The hole in the center was where the locking device was. The chest is on display at the Stagecoach Museum, Lusk, Wyoming. *(Photo: Courtesy The Lusk Herald-Aminal Caring Team.)*

It does not seem conceivable that Miner could have been tied up that long. The latest any account put the robbery was three o'clock in the afternoon. Even if the fight lasted as long as a half-hour, Davis would have left at the same time the robbers started to work on the treasure chest: 3:30. Davis said he obtained a horse from "a ranch a short way off," and was met by May, Sample, and Brown eight miles from where he obtained the horse. If Miner's "several hours" is interpreted "two hours", it would be approximately 5:30 when the box was opened. Davis had been gone for these two hours the robbers were working on the box. He had, by his own account, walked to the ranch, then ridden sixteen miles (eight miles each way). A good horse can make eight miles an hour, and it is inconceivable that the stage company would not have had good horses. If Miner had not been released until half past nine, that would mean Davis spent four hours walking to the ranch "a short way off." It is one of the many inconsistencies of the Canyon Springs robbery, but less subtle than others. Among contemporary sources only Davis stated that they arrived at Canyon Springs before the robbers left.[18]

Historical marker near Four Corners, Wyoming. The fact that the treasure coach carried as high as $150,000 out of the Black Hills has led some to believe that thousands of dollars worth of treasure was buried during the outlaws flight out of the Black Hills. *(Author's photo.)*

When Miner reached Deadwood with the news of the robbery a large possee of robber hunters left Deadwood for Canyon Springs, and for each returning posseman there was four to take his place when the stage company offered a $2,500 reward for the robbers, and 10%

of the treasure for its return.[19] One member of Scott Davis' posse returned to Deadwood early and reported that while Davis, combing the Inyan Kara country, was thought to be "off the scent" he thought deputy U.S. Marshal Seth Bullock, William Ward, June Dix and others were on the right track.[20] Bullock's posse went in the direction of Robber's Roost,[21] "a wild, broken country near Harney's Peak, and a well-known resort for horse thieves and road agents." Ward separated from the rest of the posse and was the first to strike the robber's trail. When Ward

> . . . reached the telegraph road between Custer and Deadwood, he engaged Uri Gillett,[22] a veteran frontiersman, a crack shot, an experienced trailer and, of course, a brave man, to accompany him. Reaching Newton's Fork,[23] Ward learned that two of the robbers, who were identified as Charles Carey and Frank McBride, had purchased a team and wagon of one "Frenchy" and gone on. Ward and Gillett reached Rockville[24] late Saturday night (the 28th), completely worn out. The next morning they came on, following the trail to a point about three miles south of here (Rapid City), where it crossed the Sidney road, when they came in here for fresh horses . . .[25]

Reports about the flight path of the birds between Canyon Springs and Rapid City began to arrive in Rapid City, and continued to trickle in until well into November.

"Gang cabins," like this one at Canyon City, could frequently be found "off the beaten track." *(Photo: Courtesy South Dakota State Historical Society.)*

A miner from "the Rochford district" reported that the morning after the robbery three of the robbers came "in the neighborhood" of his camp. He said that two of the three robbers were wounded; one, McBride, in the groin, and the other, described as "a tall young man, with a smooth face," that had seven buckshot wounds scattered over his breast and stomach. According to the miner, the latter was "doctored and carefully nursed," but died the following evening.[26] He claimed that he could easily locate the grave, but later efforts to do so proved fruitless.[27] Although his description of the man was vague, it was similar to the sketchy description Scott Davis gave of the man he shot.[28]

Mr. Frost's account was one of the last to be heard, but was also one of the most substantial. He was a former hunting partner of Carey's so there was little chance of error in his identification:

> . . . Frost . . . said his old partner, Carey, was in the Canyon Springs stage robbery, and that he took McBride and another one of the robbers, who was wounded in that affair, out of the country. The party called at Frost's cabin, in Rockville, and remained with him several hours. Frost was not aware of the fact at the time that his old friend had become a bandit, but was considerably puzzled all the same how he came into possession of the large amount of gold which he had on his person . . .[29]

It is little wonder that Frost was "considerably puzzled" by the large amount of gold. With two wounded robbers, Carey would have had three-fifths, or more, of the Canyon Springs booty.[30]

Jim Sherman of Newton City arrived in Rapid City with a report that added some credibility to the Rochford miner's claim that one of the robbers had died. According to Sherman:

> **two** of them stopped there and purchased supplies, **one** of them laying in the wagon, and reported to be very sick by his partner. They made a very short stay and then departed in the direction of Sheridan, as fast as their team could go.[31]

Another report, nearer to Rapid City, again mentions only two robbers, and brings us back to Ward's pursuit of the bandits:

> . . . The trail of the wagon has been easily followed. When they reached Rapid Creek, instead of hiding the trail, as they might easily have done // they drove straight across the creek at a point where the bottom was soft on either side. This must have been about daylight Sunday morning (three days after the robbery, the 29th). About 7 o'clock that morning, just as

Capt. Ward and his party were leaving Rockville, two men rode up to Evans and Loveland's store, and while one entered and bought provisions the other stood at the door as if on guard. Both were armed to the teeth. Mr. Loveland's suspicions were aroused and he started out to find Ed. Cooke and acquaint him with the circumstances, but was dissuaded therefrom by an old gas bag who was standing near and claimed to know both men, and that they were "all right" // The wagon passed Morrison's ranch some fifteen miles from here (Rapid City) about 7 o'clock that morning . . .[32]

The **Black Hills Daily Times** noted that an exchange had stated that a "smart woodpecker" could fly sixty miles a night. The **Times** dryly responded that "an ordinary road agent, it would seem, can beat a woodpecker by many miles."[33]

At Rapid City Ward and Gillette were joined in their pursuit of the robbers by Sheriff Moulton and Deputy Sheriff Steele, C. B. Stocking, "Doc" Peirce, Dr. N. C. Whitfield, and five or six others, all mounted on the "best horses" that Cook was supposed to have ready for Bullock's party.[34] Although Cook could hardly be faulted for giving them to the first party to arrive, horses, politics, "back home" electioneering by the newspapers, and bickering between the possemen later reduced the posse to shambles.

The posse made twelve miles, then decided to strike directly for the river road. When they reached the river road the driver of an inbound coach reported that he had seen the robbers, in camp, between Washta Springs and the Cheyenne River. The posse reached the springs about nine p.m., and the robbers were just ahead. It had been decided that they would lay over until midnight then mount up and ride on. Soon after they settled down "a party of six or seven men came up to the ranch from the west, who proved to be the Deadwood party headed by Seth Bullock." At 2 p.m. the combined posses resumed the chase for the robbers. As they neared the last reported camp of the robbers two men rode ahead to make a reconnoiter of the camp, to be followed by the full posse in a half hour. The advance party reported "the game gone" when the others arrived, and they spent the remainder of the night there.[35]

The next morning they were back in the saddle again — but not all going in the same direction. Sheriff Moulton and Emmett James returned to Rapid City, according to C. B. Stocking because Ward and Beaman had "commenced to snarl and growl" because the others had better horses. The **Black Hills Journal** reported that Sheriff

Moulton had to return because court was in session, but it would be well to remember that 1878 was an election year — and Sheriff Moulton was also candidate Moulton.[36]

The election also influenced the way the pursuit of the robbers was reported in Deadwood. The **Black Hills Daily Times** first reported that Sheriff Manning, in Cheyenne on official business when the robbery occurred, had left the stage at Hat Creek and organized a posse and was searching for the robbers in the direction of Fort McKinney.[37] To everyone's surprise, Sheriff Manning stepped off the stage when it arrived in Deadwood. The **Times** capitalized on the fact that Manning was about Deadwood, and reported each official, though mundane, act he performed while giving lengthy, detailed reports of candidate Seth Bullock's pursuit of the robbers. Although the posse had no one leading it, to the **Times** it was "Seth Bullock's posse."[38]

While the newspapers carried on the electioneering at home, the posse learned that the night they spent at the reported robber camp, the robbers had crossed the Cheyenne River. On the hill above the river one of the posse said they had gone far enough without a "Captain," and nominated Ed Cook. His motion carried and "Captain" Cook performed his first official act. He said that he had hired, and was, therefore, responsible for, a number of horses. "Captain" Cook then ordered back "Doc" Peirce, Gillette, and Stocking, who were all mounted on horses Cook felt he was responsible for. Stocking later complained in a letter to the **Black Hills Daily Times** that "when we started, horses were of no value" but "when we were about to capture the wagon they concluded that we three would be in the way." It was reported that "Doc" left "reluctantly."[39] Although he was not a candidate for the office of Sheriff in 1878, he won the job in the 1880 by a plurality of one.[40]

There was evidently politics at work within the posse for Cook to have been elected "Captain" over a man in a higher position within the stage company, and over Deputy U.S. Marshal Seth Bullock. Although the number of Rapid Citians in the posse could have eliminated Bullock and Ward, both from Deadwood, it is interesting that Cook wasn't made "Captain" until after Sheriff Moulton had returned to Rapid City. The suggestion was apparently made by one of Cook's cronies who felt Ward's position would be available after Voorhees learned Ward had failed to accompany the Moniter as far as he had been instructed to. The campaigning was being done in Rapid City and Deadwood, but the politicing exceeded any county boundaries. Indeed, the **Black Hills Daily Times,** October 30, 1878, printed a letter from "Ward's Friend," in which he stated: ". . . it was known by good responsible citizens in Deadwood that Mr. Ward was to be dismissed . . ."

At Deadman's Creek a "council of war" was held and a wagon chartered for the Deadwood men to ride in. A cold rain struck about the same time a dim camp fire was seen in the distance. A halt was ordered and two men rode off to investigate. The remainder of the posse waited for orders, and when it was discovered to be a freighter's camp, the order to move on came. The party rode on to within two miles of Mitchell Creek, when, according to Dr. Whitfield:

> . . . it being very dark, nothing could be distinguished ten feet
> from the road. As the cavalcade crossed a little sag, a horse to
> the left of us was heard to neigh. The call was noted by our
> men, and after driving on about a mile, a halt was made.[41]

From the **Black Hills Daily Times** account, written after an interview with Seth Bullock:

> . . . Cook . . . concluded to reconnoiter the camp of the high-
> waymen . . . and soon returned with the information that the
> men they wanted were in the brush where the horse was heard
> to winnow. Hereupon Bullock and some others were in favor
> of surrounding the camp, shooting the horses, and by keeping
> a fire on the wagon, recover the treasure, besides setting the
> robbers afoot, but Cook overruled the camp, thinking that
> the robbers were ignorant of their presence and would not
> start until daybreak . . .[42]

It was a good scheme, but poorly executed. At daybreak, according to Dr. Whitfield:

> . . . A grand charge was ordered all along the line and the old
> wagon was taken in, but the birds had flown and the nest was
> cold. One old coat, some bacon, flour, two belts with car-
> tridges, a gun case, pistol scabbard, one axe, some shelled
> corn, a heavy double harness and some other articles were
> found on the field . . .[43]

The disgruntled posse went to the stage station on Mitchell Creek and had breakfast. Bullock, Beaman, and Deputy Sheriff Steele were forced to return, while the six who could find fresh horses continued the pursuit. Ward and Cook started for Pierre, while J. H. Burns, Dr. Whitfield, and two employees of the stage company followed the trail of the robbers "across the plains in the direction of the Red Cloud Agency."[44]

They followed, lost, and found the trail of the robbers several times during the course of the next few days. Riders matching the descriptions of Carey and McBride had asked for directions to various locations, most of them sites along the Bad River. After several days of a "flapjacks and alkali water diet," the four rode to Pierre then started for home with one prisoner.[45]

Ward and Cook had continued to Pierre. At Pierre they learned that a man answering the description of one of the robbers had recently crossed the Missouri River. His description was sent out to points along the river, and he was quickly arrested at Ft. Thompson.[46] The **Black Hills Daily Times** correspondent in Rapid City reported:

> . . . From what I hear, he was the advance guard of those who were in the wagon, keeping in advance of them most of the time, riding into all camps they saw on the route. He was seen by a great many persons, and all describe him as being just ahead of the wagon, and as one of the party.[47]

The prisoner proved to be Andy Gouch, known around Deadwood as "Red Cloud." According to John McClintock, who knew him only as "Red Cloud," Gouch had stolen a horse from Blanche White, whom he described as "a notorious woman of the town," and then rode hell-bent for Canyon Springs when the Moniter left Deadwood the day of the robbery.[48]

When they arrived at the camp the robbers had deserted prior to their daybreak charge Dr. Whitfield related:

> . . . although I was called a fool, I stopped and searched the vicinity of their camp thoroughly, being finally rewarded by the bullion I brought in hidden in tall weeds and grass . . .[49]

The bullion and retort found by Dr. Whitfield weighed about 650 ounces, and was valued between $10,000 and $12,000. Dr. Whitfield received a reward of $1,100 from the stage company.[50] How much his pursuit of the Canyon Springs stage robbers had to do with it is indeterminable, but he was elected county coroner and to the House of Representatives in the November election.[51]

In Cheyenne many residents had turned out to view the Moniter when it arrived, "still spotted with the blood of Campbell, and riddled with bullets."[52]

In Deadwood the funeral for Hugh Campbell had been well attended, and Dr. Babcock reported Gale Hill was "doing well." Officers were scurrying about "trying to find out where some of the boys of the town made their raise of funds"[53] and the **Black Hills Daily**

Times reported that it seemed "to be the intention of the authorities to take in every suspected road agent, horse thief, and bold bad man in the country." Two officers arrived with "Tony Pastor" and Charles Hager in tow, "the former a noted horse thief, and the latter a keeper of a ranch at the old crossing on the Custer Trail." Hager had been arrested on the strength of a letter which had been found under the Moniter the day of the robbery. The letter, from a "notorious woman at Lead," promised that she would "send a girl out to his ranch who knew her business and would keep still." As for his companion, George Howard, being "Tony Pastor" was enough to get him cinched. Pastor admitted that maybe he had been out on a horse stealing expedition, but denied any involvement in the robbery and both were later released.[54]

Robberies had previously been attributed to cowboys, tenderfeet, and broke miners, which caused the **Times** to wonder: if they were responsible, "in the name of all that's good, how would we fare with a few old professionals on the road?"

Stragglers from various posses drifted into Deadwood and Rapid City, and Gough was prevented from escaping by an observant deputy sheriff. According to McClintock, **Gough** was sentenced to serve two years in the penitentiary for grand larceny.[55]

From Cheyenne the stage company sent out circulars with the descriptions of Carey and McBride:

Charles Carey, 27 years old; light complexion; brown hair; if any beard, little sandy; weight 175; six feet high; has new large Ulster overcoat, a little gray; carries Winchester rifle and Winchester cartridge belt; pock-marks on each side of his nose; rode gray pony, unshod; was formerly a scout for Gen. Custer.

Frank McBride, with Carey, is a small man, with small features; small feet; light brown hair; light mustache and goatee; weight, 145 pounds; 24 years old; very sharp eyes; supposed to be wounded; was riding dark sorrel pony, baldfaced, blind in one eye, and barefoot.[56]

The description of Frank McBride may have been unnecessary. The **Black Hills Daily Times** reported that there was "tolerable good evidence" that he had died in the Missouri River region.[57] Richard Hughes didn't think so, but neither McBride or Charles Carey were ever heard from again.[58]

Ed Cook returned home from Pierre while William Ward, with a good lead on a suspect, continued on to Atlantic, Iowa.

Sol Star of Star & Bullock hardware store, Deadwood, D.T., minded the store while partner Seth Bullock hunted outlaws. (Photo: Courtesy South Dakota State Historical Society.)

Richard B. Hughes, early Black Hills newshound. *(Photo: South Dakota State Historical Society.)*

1. Richard B. Hughes (Agnes Wright Spring, ed.), **Pioneer Years in the Black Hills,** p. 252.
2. **Cheyenne Daily Leader,** May 16, 1878. Ironically, just five days before the Canyon Springs robbery, the **Black Hills Daily Times** noted that the second iron clad coach had just been finished.
3. **Cheyenne Daily Leader,** April 13, 1878. Brown and Willard's **The Black Hills Trails,** p. 263 stated the treasure coach carried as high as $140,000 while Scott Davis stated the amount of $300,000 was "frequently" carried in his account which was given to the **Lusk Herald,** February 25, 1932.
4. Leander P. Richardson, "A Trip to the Black Hills," **Scribners,** Vol. XIII (April, 1877), p. 756.
5. **Lusk Herald,** op. cit.; Hughes, op. cit., p. 252.
6. **Lusk Herald,** op. cit. Placement as given by Scott Davis. Among his contemporaries, Hughes, op. cit., p. 253, placed Davis on the boot with Barnett, while McClintock, p. 214, puts Campbell next to Barnett. The **Black Hills Journal,** October 5, 1878, concurs with Davis' seating arrangement.
7. Agnes Wright Spring, **The Cheyenne and Black Hills Stage and Express Routes,** p. 266.
8. **Lusk Herald,** op. cit. In his statement to Luke Voorhees, Miner did not indicate that anyone else was present. Brown and Willard, op. cit., p. 263, state that another man happened to be there, and they were both tied up as Miner stated. Hughes, op. cit., p. 252, states a special messenger from Deadwood was also there. John S. McClintock, **Pioneer Days in the Black Hills,** p. 213, mentions only the stock tender whom he erroneously identified as "Stuttering Dick" Wright. **Black Hills Journal,** op. cit., states Zimmer, a messenger "who had just reached the station" was there.
9. **Lusk Herald,** op. cit.; **Black Hills Journal,** op. cit.; **Cheyenne Daily Leader,** September 28, 1878.
10. **Black Hills Journal,** October 5, 1878.

11.   Smith's wound has been variously reported. The **Black Hills Journal,**
      op. cit., stated he was injured as given. Davis' account stated he was
      shot in the side of the head, but states Campbell was not wounded
      first. The **Cheyenne Daily Leader,** September 28, 1878, stated Smith
      was "slightly hurt by a ball grazing the top of his head. McClintock,
      op. cit., does not mention Smith at all. Brown and Willard, op. cit.,
      p. 264, states Smith was struck by a splinter from the top of the
      coach, which was not iron plated, and thought he had been shot.
      Hughes, op. cit., p. 254, stated Smith wasn't wounded at all. It
      should be noted that the authors of the last two accounts were not
      there at the time, while Davis, who was, stated, "We supposed he
      was dead," and Brown, who arrived a short time later, indicated that
      he had been wounded — if not shot.

12.   **Lusk Herald,** op. cit.; **Black Hills Journal,** op. cit. McClintock, op.
      cit., p. 214, states Campbell was "killed outright," but had Camp-
      bell seated on the boot. It would have been impossible for the ball to
      pass through his head and wound Smith if he were seated on the
      boot, which he wasn't. Hughes, op. cit., p. 253, stated Campbell
      died within a few hours which would somewhat agree with Davis' ac-
      count, in that he lived long enough to leave the coach before receiv-
      ing the fatal wound.

13.   **Lusk Herald,** op. cit.

14.   **Black Hills Journal,** op. cit.; It is interesting to note that of his con-
      temporaries, only Scott Davis fails to state Gale Hill wounded one of
      the robbers, and at the same time is the only one to claim they ar-
      rived in time to engage the robbers in a second fight, during which
      one of them was wounded. McBride identification from **Black Hills
      Daily Times,** October 15, 1878, and others.

15.   **Lusk Herald,** op. cit.

16.   **Black Hills Journal,** op. cit.; **Lusk Herald,** op. cit.

17.   **Lusk Herald,** op. cit. The **Cheyenne Daily Leader,** September 28,
      timed the opening of the safe at "a short time."

18.   **Lusk Herald,** op. cit.; **Cheyenne Daily Leader,** October 2, 1878;
      Brown and Willard, op. cit., p. 267; **Black Hills Journal,** op. cit.

19.   The reward offered was $500, upon conviction, for each of the five
      robbers and 10% of the loot recovered to be pro rated, the total
      possible reward for recovery being $2,700. While the **Cheyenne
      Daily Leader** headed their copy of the reward offering "$2,500
      Reward," the **Black Hills Daily Times** used the heading "$5,000
      Reward."

20.   **Black Hills Daily Times,** September 30, 1878.

21.   Not to be confused with the "Robber's Roost" station in Wyoming, D.
      Boone May, proprietor.

22.   Uriah Gillette.

23.   Northwest of Hill City.

24.   The community was known as Rockerville, while the post office was
      officially Rockville. The name of the post office was changed to
      Rockerville March 1, 1879.

25.   **Black Hills Journal,** October 5, 1878.

26.   **Black Hills Journal,** November 16, 1878; **Black Hills Daily Times,**
      November 8, 1878.

27.   **Black Hills Daily Times,** November 8, 1878.

28.   Ibid.

29.   **Black Hills Daily Times,** November 21, 1878.

30.   It is quite possible that they had more than three-fifths of the loot.
      Albert Spears, later captured, said that the spoils were divided in

his absence, and he had been told they "didn't make much of a haul."

31. **Black Hills Daily Times,** October 3, 1878. Sheridan Lake now covers what was Sheridan.

32. **Black Hills Daily Times,** October 4, 1878.

33. **Black Hills Daily Times,** September 28, 1878.

34. **Black Hills Journal,** October 5, 1878. (Jack Gilmer had ordered the horses held in readiness for Bullock's party. **Black Hills Daily Times,** September 30, 1878.)

35. **Black Hills Journal,** October 5, 1878. (Bullock's party struck the trail at Newton City. **Black Hills Daily Times,** October 3, 1878.)

36. **Black Hills Daily Times,** October 15 and 17, 1878; **Black Hills Journal,** October 17, 1878.

37. **Black Hills Daily Times,** September 30, 1878.

38. Ibid. The correction appeared in a small brevity column titled "City and Vicinity" adjoining the erroneous information. One needs to read only a few days following this to discern the difference in the reporting of the two men's activities.

39. **Black Hills Journal,** October 12, 1878; **Black Hills Daily Times,** October 15, 1878.

40. **Black Hills Journal,** November 9, 1878 and November 20, 1880. "Doc" won the election, in which Moulton was not a candidate, over George Metcalf.

41. **Black Hills Journal,** October 12, 1878.

42. **Black Hills Daily Times,** October 3, 1878. The **Black Hills Journal,** October 12, 1878, and this account which also came from a posseman support each other in the details of the posse's chase and the events.

43. **Black Hills Journal,** October 12, 1878.

44. Ibid. Although Dr. Whitfield did not mention J. H. Burns as a member of this posse, the **Black Hills Daily Times,** October 17, 1878, stated: "J. H. Burns was placed in charge of a party of three men . . ." and identified Dr. Whitfield by name as one of the three.

45. **Black Hills Journal,** October 12 and 17, 1878; **Black Hills Daily Times,** October 17, 1878.

46. **Black Hills Daily Times,** October 15 and 17, 1878.

47. **Black Hills Daily Times,** October 12, 1878.

48. Ibid.; John S. McClintock, op. cit., pp. 213 and 215.

49. **Black Hills Journal,** October 12, 1878. Although various accounts state that Gouch later told Voorhees where part of the loot was buried, I wonder if this isn't a reference to that found by Dr. Whitfield. Gouch was present on the return, and would have been in the party when it was found.

50. Ibid.; Agnes Wright Spring, op. cit., p. 273.

51. **Black Hills Journal,** November 9, 1878.

52. **Cheyenne Daily Leader,** October 2, 1878 and May 5, 1880.

53. **Black Hills Daily Times,** October 3, and 7, 1878.

54. **Black Hills Daily Times,** October 3, 1878.

55. **Black Hills Journal,** November 16, 1878; McClintock, op. cit., pp. 213 and 215.

56. **Black Hills Daily Times,** October 16, 1878. Hughes, op. cit., pp. 249-250, is probably correct in stating General Crook.

57. **Black Hills Daily Times,** October 15 and 16, 1878.

58. Hughes, op. cit., p. 258. One rumor was afloat for a while that McBride was "in Kansas and getting well." **Black Hills Daily Times,** November 14, 1878.

THE ARREST AND "ESCAPE" OF "DUCK" GOODALE

The community of Atlantic, Iowa, was shocked when Thomas Jefferson "Duck" Goodale was arrested on the charge of being a Black Hills road agent involved in the Canyon Springs robbery. "Duck," the son of Almond Goodale "one of the old and respected citizens of Cass County," had returned to Atlantic from the Black Hills the morning of October 10, 1878.[1] The Goodale family had lived in Atlantic for over twenty-five years where the senior Goodale farmed and was a dealer of agricultural implements.[2] "Duck," the eldest of seven children, had married in 1873.[3] The **Atlantic Telegraph** and the Cass County Census for 1880 both indicate that one child, Thomas, was born but neither offers any information about the mother. Both sources indicate that the child lived with his grandparents.[4]

William Ward had preceded Goodale to Atlantic, and Goodale was arrested October 13 "after several days of watching and manuevering by the officers." How Ward had preceded him is not clear. First reports stated that Ward was in Atlantic looking for another man when Goodale came under suspicion, but later reports said that one of his accomplices had provided the names and hometowns of the others after he was "strung up and lowered four times in succession."[5]

Contrary to most hometown newspapers of accused Black Hills road agents, the **Atlantic Telegraph** didn't rally to Goodale's defense. It impartially reported that:

The evidence against young Goodale consists of the finding of the following property substantially in his possession: a gold brick weighing 248.87 ounces; 986 grains of gold dust; (both amounts aggregating $4,400); one lady's gold watch and chain; two silver watches; a seven set diamond ring; two plain gold rings; one shotgun; and two revolvers (one having an ivory handle) . . .[6]

The gold brick and the three watches were found in the safe of the senior Goodale in a leading Cass County bank.[7] John S. McClintock called Ward's story about happening to see the brick in the window of his father's bank "a great cock and bull story," and said he knew Goodale "too well to classify him as an arrant fool."[8] The **Atlantic Telegraph** made no mention of the gold being on display in a bank window, nor was Goodale's father a banker for that matter. The rest of the plunder was found in "Duck's" possession when he was arrested at his father's house.[9]

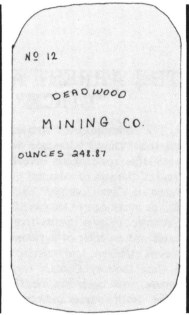

The **Atlantic Telegraph,** October 16, 1878, gave a diagram of the gold brick, "showing its exact size at the top." It weighed about twenty pounds, and was "very bright from handling and from carrying in a bag or satchel."

When "Duck" placed the gold and watches in his father's safe, he told him that he had sold a mining claim in the Black Hills. The **Telegraph** said the story, "too gauzy to stand inspection, was readily believed by the fond father." It was, however, far more plausible than the story Goodale told Ward. Goodale told Ward that he, with several others, had come upon a band of robbers in a secreted spot. Their sudden appearance had unnerved the robbers and caused them to run away, leaving behind the large amount of booty they had evidently stolen. The party figured they had as much right to it as anyone else, and divided it up among themselves.[10]

Goodale was taken to Des Moines on a writ of habeas corpus for his preliminary hearing.[11] Upon his arrival in Des Moines he was immediately taken to jail where he was questioned by a deputy sheriff and a **State Register** reporter. When they entered his cell, Goodale turned his back on them and gazed intently out the window. He answered the deputy's questions "rather reluctantly," then turned around "in a half reckless manner" and sat down on his cot. The reporter questioned him about his whereabouts when the robbery was committed, and the questions gradually grew harder:

Reporter: When did you first see Mr. Ward . . .?

Goodale: About four days ago.

Reporter: Is the story true which you told him in regard to your possession of the bullion?

Goodale: What did I tell him?

(Here the reporter repeated the story about Goodale and his party having frightened away the gang of robbers.)

Goodale: Yes, sir, that is true.

Reporter: Why did you tell your father that you procured it by selling a claim you owned in the Hills?

Goodale: I told him that to blind him. I had to tell him something, you know.

Goodale admitted that it would be difficult for him to establish his innocence, but didn't waver from the story he told Ward. The story the reporter had to remind him of. Goodale appeared to take little interest in his case and "cares little about his condition." As the visitors were about to leave, Goodale lit a cigar, strolled to the window and "smoked away in an indifferent manner."[12]

Iowa's Governor Gear granted Wyoming's requisition for Goodale, and on October 22 he was returned to Atlantic. He was visited that night by his parents, son, and other relatives. The next morning Ward, Goodale, and A. S. Churchill, an attorney hired by his father, left for Cheyenne.[13] At the Council Bluffs depot shackles were riveted on his legs by a railroad blacksmith.[14] A few minutes before seven p.m., three miles west of Central City, Nebraska,

"Duck" Goodale's escape was detected. Except for their individual movements William Ward and A. S. Churchill told the same story. Churchill said:

> He (Churchill) and Ward had been sitting together in one seat, Goodale sat in the seat in front of them. Goodale asked Ward for permission to go to the water closet. Ward got up and walked with Goodale to the closet; Goodale went into the closet and Ward stepped out of the car onto the platform. Presently Ward came into the car and looked into the closet, and seeing that Goodale was not there, at once hollered with great force, "Churchill, Duck's gone!" Mr. Churchill says the escape frightened him almost as much as it did Ward, and he at once jerked the bell rope to stop the train.[15]

The train immediately backed up to Central City. District Court was in session there, and Ward, with the sheriff and a posse of men, searched for Goodale but were not able to find any trace of him. There was no timber in the area where Goodale escaped, about three miles from the Platte River, but the area was covered by tall grass.[16] Goodale's shackles were found in the water closet.[17] He was wearing heavy calf-skin boots and some thought that he slipped the shackles off after he removed his boots; others, that he had quietly sawed them off with a burglar's saw.[18] It may have been, however, as the **Central City Courier** stated: "It is hinted at pretty strongly that Goodale never reached Central City." The **Courier** found it "passing strange" that:

> . . . a man weighing 165 pounds, heavily shackled, could throw himself from a car window, the train going at the rate of twenty-two miles an hour, and escape in an open country thoroughly searched over by a body of mounted men . . .[19]

The **Kearney Press** of November 6, 1878 reported that Luke Voorhees was satisfied that Goodale never escaped by jumping from the train at all. Voorhees felt that Goodale's escape was accomplished either by his walking through the door of the train and stepping off on the platform on the other side when the train left Central City, or Goodale had climbed to the roof where an accomplice was stationed to assist him. Voorhees stopped short of accusing Ward of complicity, "but thinks it a case of gross carelessness, if nothing else, and has discharged him (Ward)."[20]

Luke Voorhees was in Atlantic October 28 to pick up the loot that Goodale had had. It was rumored that Ward had been the recipient of $3,000 for letting Goodale escape, but this was never proven, nor were charges brought against him.[21] The Goodale family, by 1884, had moved to Nebraska.[22] It is quite possible that "Duck" later rejoined them, for he was never recaptured.

En route to Cheyenne, Luke Voorhees stopped at Ogallala, Nebraska, to discuss the Canyon Springs robbery with M. F. Leach. The subject of Al Spears and his sudden wealth quite naturally came up.[23]

1. *Atlantic* (Iowa) **Telegraph,** October 16, 1878.
2. **Atlantic Telegraph,** October 23, 1878.
3. 1870 Iowa Census, Roll 380, p. 41; 1880 Iowa Census, Roll 331, p. 10; **Cass County Iowa Marriages,** compiled by the D.A.R., Vol. 57. The **Black Hills Journal,** October 26, 1878 stated: "Dug Goodale . . . left his wife . . . because of some misunderstanding . . ."
4. **Atlantic Telegraph,** October 23, 1878.
5. **Atlantic Telegraph,** October 16, 1878.
6. **Atlantic Telegraph,** October 16, 1878.
7. **Atlantic Telegraph,** October 23, 1878.
8. John S. McClintock, **Pioneer Days in the Black Hills,** pp. 214-5. McClintock, like most of his contemporaries, corrupted Goodale's nickname of "Duck" to "Doug," or "Dug."
9. **Atlantic Telegraph,** October 16, 1878.
10. **Atlantic Telegraph,** October 23, 1878.
11. Ibid.
12. Ibid.
13. Ibid.
14. **Black Hills Daily Times,** undated article in author's file, quoting the **Sidney Plaindealer.**
15. **Atlantic Telegraph,** October 30, 1878.
16. Ibid.
17. **Atlantic Telegraph,** October 30, 1878 merely states that Goodale "had shackles on his ankles, but none on his wrists" and does not elaborate about where the shackles were found. The **Black Hills Daily Times,** undated in the author's files, quotes the Sidney **Plaindealer** in stating the shackles were found in the water closet.
18. **Atlantic Teiegraph,** October 30, 1878.
19. **Central City** (Nebraksa) **Courier,** October 31, 1878.
20. **Kearney** (Nebraska) **Press,** November 6, 1878.
21. **Atlantic Telegraph,** October 30, 1878; Agnes Wright Spring, **The Cheyenne-Deadwood Stage and Express Routes,** p. 274.
22. History of Cass County (Iowa), p. 573.
23. **Cheyenne Daily Leader,** November 2, 1878.

ALBERT SPEARS

Leach told Voorhees that Albert Spears, a man that he suspected of being one of the Canyon Springs robbers, had recently visited Ogallala and had "exhibited . . . a quantity of jewelry, several pistols and a considerable amount of bullion." It was decided that Leach should arrest Spears if he made another appearance in Ogallala.[1]

When Spears went to the Black Hills, about a year before the Canyon Springs robbery, he left a trunk in Cheyenne with a friend. After the robbery, Spears wrote to the friend and asked that it be sent to him. Leach obtained the letter and learned the whereabouts of his suspect. One report stated that Leach arrested Spears in Grand Island, where he caught him in the act of disposing of some of his loot.[2] Other, more feasible and probably more reliable accounts, stated that Spears was arrested at the farm of his employer, near Wood River. Along this line, the report said that Spears **had** been in Grand Island and had sold $840 worth of gold dust there. Both accounts state that Spears was about to draw his revolver, but looked up and saw he was covered by Leach's "murderous looking revolver." Those who knew Spears said they did not think that he could be taken alive.[3]

Most of Spears' share of the loot was recovered at the time of his arrest. A quantity of jewelry was found and the gun that had been taken from Gale Hill at the time of the robbery. About $500 was found in his possession, and Spears said that he had loaned $400 of it to a farmer without security, which the farmer denied.[4]

Spears was taken to Cheyenne and when they arrived, on November 1, 1878. Leach said that Spears had made a "clean breast" of the whole affair. Spears said that the Canyon Springs robbery was his first and last stage robbery. He said that he was "coaxed into it by the others," and as he had been pretty hard up all summer it didn't take much coaxing. The **Cheyenne Daily Leader** reported that Spears' name had been "in the possession of the officers" for several months, that he was a cattle thief, hard customer, and his statement about it being his first venture "can safely be heard with a reasonable degree of allowance."[5] As it happened, when they arrived, two women were there to inquire about recovering the value of their jewelry which had been stolen during the Canyon Springs robbery. They were asked to describe the jewelry and it was the same jewelry that had been found on Spears.[6]

Spears said that he was born in Gibson County, Indiana, and had been employed by the American Bridge Company when the new bridge was built over Dale Creek, Wyoming. After that he went to the Black Hills and spent most of his time hunting. It was during this time that he "fell in" with the others. Spears said that the loot had been divided in his absence and he had been told they "didn't make much of a haul."[7]

Albert Spears worked on the construction of the steel bridge which replaced the one shown. This bridge, constructed entirely of wood, was 125 feet high and 500 feet long. It was erected in thirty working days. *(Photo: Courtesy Union Pacific Railroad Museum.)*

Spears told Voorhees that he had buried the gold under about three feet of dirt near the farm where he had been employed. The next day, after about a half-hour digging, Voorhees found the gold, valued at about $4,000.[8]

Spears said that he had travelled as far as North Platte, Nebraska, with "Duck" Goodale. From there he went to Wood River where he found employment.[9]

Although he claimed to have only acted as a look-out for the gang, he later confessed that he had killed Campbell. On November 27, 1878 Spears was sentenced to life in the penitentiary. He served his time in the Nebraska penitentiary under the name of "Albert Spurs," and received a pardon September 25, 1889.[10]

1. **Cheyenne Daily Leader,** November 2, 1878; **Cheyenne Daily Sun,** November 5, 1878; **Atlantic Telegraph,** November 13, 1878.
2. **Black Hills Journal,** November 9, 1878. **Cheyenne Daily Leader,** op. cit.
3. Ibid.; **Atlantic Telegraph,** op. cit.
4. **Black Hills Journal,** op. cit.
5. **Cheyenne Daily Leader,** op. cit.
6. **Black Hills Journal,** op. cit.; **Atlantic Telegraph,** op. cit.
7. **Atlantic Telegraph,** op. cit. **Cheyenne Daily Leader,** op. cit.; **Cheyenne Daily Sun,** November 2, 1878.
8. **Cheyenne Daily Sun,** November 4, 1878.
9. **Atlantic Telegraph,** op. cit.
10. "Record, Description and History of Convicts in Penitentiaries of Wyoming Territory," entry for Albert Spears; Agnes Wright Spring, **The Cheyenne-Black Hills Stage and Express Routes,** p. 280.

IN SEARCH OF JIM McCLOUD

With scant knowledge of Jim McCloud, a noted Wyoming outlaw, I began an eight year search for answers to two questions which seemed quite simple: Who was Jim McCloud and what became of him?

From the Wyoming State Archives, Museums, and Historical Department (WSAMHD), I obtained photocopies of newspaper articles concerning McCloud's involvement in the Buffalo post office burglary, the Horn-McCloud attempt to escape from the Cheyenne jail, and several items which attracted my attention. From the **Buffalo Bulletin**, November 19, 1903:

> It turns out . . . Jim McCloud once served time in this state. He was sent up from Converse county . . . and was discharged at the expiration of his term in 1892. He was then known as John Dale.

More intriguing, however, was an article from the **Wyoming Tribune**, February 11, 1907, which said, in part:

> This afternoon he was taken south on his way to the federal prison at Leavenworth, Kansas from which he escaped in 1898 . . . McCloud, whose real name is William Pierce . . .

Not all of the information from the newspaper accounts was correct, but out of necessity had to be documented either as correct or as incorrect. The **Buffalo Bulletin**, January 21, 1904 gave the following editorial comment concerning Jim McCloud:

> It is a little difficult to see why an habitual criminal, with a term or two in the Wyoming penitentiary, an escape from the penitentiary of Kansas, a strong moral probability of guilt

of the Minnick murder, of participation in the Union Pacific robbery, and the certainty of his active participation in the Horn-McCloud escape to his discredit, should not get the limit.

A letter to the Converse County Clerk of Courts revealed that no John Dale had ever been prosecuted in Converse County, but only one Dale had — James Dale. Their file on James Dale was small, but provided the date of his conviction, length of sentence, and the date of the crime for which he was convicted. With the information from the court records, I wrote to the Converse County Library, and Librarian Margretta Perry copied the articles concerning James Dale for me from **Bill Barlow's Budget.** Ida Wozny of the WSAMHD located and mailed me copies of the prison records for James Dale. She had earlier mailed the records for Jim McCloud. The records were so dissimilar that I wondered if the guard's memory had been in error. Meanwhile, a letter from Duane Shillinger, Warden, Wyoming State Penitentiary, contained the following information:

. . . a search of our records revealed the photo and information on Mr. McCloud . . . His prison photo is enclosed . . .

The letter also contained a reference to an alias of James Dah. This, I was sure, was Dale, but not conclusive enough to prove the fact that James Dale and Jim McCloud were the same person. I had earlier located a photo of James Dale in the files of the WSAMHD, and sent my photo of Jim McCloud to Paula West and Ida Wozny to compare with theirs of James Dale. Mrs. Wozny replied:

You will be pleased to find your opinion is correct. James Dale and James McCloud are the same person. I have enclosed a record from the Wyoming State Penitentiary proving this.

The alias was listed as James Dale. It did look like James Dah, but it was Dale. Jim McCloud's criminal career as James Dale was complete.

Frequent letters to Leavenworth Penitentiary went unanswered, while the Leavenworth Historical Society was unable to provide any information. Finally one of my periodic letters inquiring about Jim McCloud was returned with the notation:

Rec'd 4-24-1896 Reg #493 Wm Pierce 5 years B&E p.o. Rel. 3-30-1909

The unidentified source provided no further information, but had provided another clue: William Pierce. And another question: Was Jim McCloud really William Pierce, or was Pierce, like Dale, an alias of Jim McCloud? Another letter to Leavenworth, but this letter inquired about William Pierce, Reg. #493. Although I was convinced that his real name was Jim McCloud, which later proved to be correct, the query about William Pierce brought, in part, this information about William Pierce from D. L. Wilbourne, Records Department Manager, Leavenworth Penitentiary:

> Our records indicate that Mr. Pierce, Reg. No. 493 was received at this institution on April 24, 1896 to serve 5 years for Breaking into Post Office. He escaped on May 12, 1897 . . . He had aliases of Jim McCloud, Jim McLeod, Driftwood Jim, J. W. McCloud and Jim William McCloud . . . His last commitment was on February 20, 1944 . . . transferred to the Federal Correctional Institution, Seagoville, Texas, on July 17, 1945 . . . our records were transfered to FCI, Seagoville . . .

The letter also contained information about five convictions previously unknown to me. The helpful letter, however, ended with the discouraging note that all records probably had been destroyed.

Other leads were also being pursued simultaniously. I had learned, for instance, that Jim McCloud had not killed Ben Minnick as the **Buffalo Bulletin** had suggested. A good deal of information was acquired about Charles W. (William?) Pierce, an escapee from the Kansas State Penitentiary at Lansing. Then an early history of escapes from Lansing revealed that this Pierce had never been recaptured.

A letter to the Federal Correctional Institution received an acknowledgement with the information that my request had been forwarded to the General Consul. An acknowledgement from the General Consul's office was followed by a thick envelope from the Bureau of Prison's South Central Regional Office. From the cover letter:

> Attached are copies of Mr. McCloud's records during his incarceration at FCI . . . i.e., photo, FBI rap sheet; Certificate of Release; Conditional Release Statement; Progress Report; and Admission Summaries. . .

Before me lay twenty-five pages of prison records for Jim McCloud and a photograph of him taken in 1944. Jim McCloud had had two criminal careers, and from the records, had been able to conceal his career as James Dale and William Pierce from Leavenworth officials. There was no information about him after his release from

FCI, except he planned to return to Anadarko, Oklahoma and the name of his parole advisor, Watt Carruth.

Larry Jochims of the Kansas State Historical Society had searched the Leavenworth newspapers of the time of the escape, and was unable to find any information. Mr. Jochims then searched the **Topeka Daily Capital** and located an article about the escape in the May 14, 1897 newspaper.

From previous information from Leavenworth Penitentiary a letter with one question was sent to the National Archives and Records Service office in St. Louis, Missouri. Although he had been sentenced at Topeka, and accounts had been written which stated he had burglarized the Topeka post office, this was erroneous. The one question letter resulted in a telephone call which stated that the post office he had burglarized as William Pierce was the Ulysses, Kansas post office.

From the Leavenworth-FCI records various leads were pursued. His friend and parole advisor Watt Carruth, had died. However, his widow mailed me Mr. Carruth's photograph and a synopsis of his thirty year law enforcement career. From Huntsville Prison, only the confirmation that Jim McCloud had served time there as Jim McLeod was available. From the Western District of Oklahoma Probation Office came the information that his records were sent to their Archives in 1961, and had since been destroyed. Since the time his prison records (photocopies) had been received the originals were destroyed. Attempts to learn if his sister was still living, to find someone who remembers him, and to find further aliases that he may have used have been fruitless.

From the time I learned that he was residing in Anadarko, Oklahoma at the time of his last arrest, I attempted to learn if he had died there. Out of desperation I mailed a letter addressed to "Any Funeral Home", Anadarko, Oklahoma. Jeanette Prather answered my letter for the Smith Funeral Home. Her letter contained the date of death, place of death, date of internment, and a form with which to obtain a certified copy of a death certificate for Jim McCloud.

From the sources cited here, and in the article which follows comes the story of Jim McCloud, noted Wyoming outlaw.

JIM McCLOUD

It was 8:35 the morning of June 4, 1946 when the old man boarded the bus at the Dallas, Texas, bus depot. The old man's emaciated features silently told of the countless years, nearly a third of his lifetime, that he had spent in prison; but no one listened. Years ago, in one prison cell or another, he had left all hope behind; but there was no one left to care. Glasses aided his once eagle-sharp eyes; he was going blind. One of his legs that had carried him ever so swiftly down the streets of Cheyenne during an attempted jailbreak with cellmate Tom Horn had been amputated just below the knee. A peg had occupied its place for years. They had been captured and Horn had cursed him and called him a coward.

Recent memories, prohibition . . . Huntsville . . . Leavenworth . . . left little room for earlier, more pleasant memories . . . his mother . . . sister Jenny . . . the wide open spaces of Wyoming. Even the pleasant memories had carried a high price. His mother had died while he was in his teens. Sister Jenny had severed their relationship as he drifted from one prison to another. Wyoming's open spaces were twice reduced to the confines of a prison yard.

Old age, stone walls, and time had allowed him to keep only the deftness of his hands from the decades past when he had known most of the long riders in Wyoming. He had known them well; he had ridden with them. He had been one of them. The old man, now termed a "habitual petty offender" by prison officials, was Jim McCloud.

Jim William McCloud was born into the life that he could never accept, or really understand, May 12, 1879 in Rhea County, Tennessee. He was the first of two children born to Jacob and Harriet Mc-Cloud who farmed 120 acres of marginal economic circumstances in rural Rhea County. Young Jim McCloud was a frequent truant, exhibited a "boys will be boys" deliquency but was never in serious trouble. Sometime between 1890 and 1896 (he gave conflicting dates), the McCloud home was broken with the death of his mother. She had been a devoted parent and her death had a devastating effect upon him. He soon lost what little interest he had in school, the family farm, and life in general. He eventually left Tennessee to escape the terrible loneliness his mother's death had left. He wandered into Kansas where he assumed the alias William Pierce and committed the first crime that can be documented.[1]

On the night of January 13, 1896 the Ulysses, Kansas, post office was burglarized. The burglars were apparently professionals. They had brought a 3/8 inch drill bit with them and stole the remainder of the tools they used from the blacksmith shop. Once the burglars were inside the combination store-post office, they broke the locks off the front and back doors: an escape route, it was thought, had they been detected. The safe was then carried to a nearby warehouse where a hole was drilled into the top of it. The hole was filled with powder and fired. Those who heard the one o'clock in the morning explosion, including the postmaster's wife, looked out but could see nothing, and returned to bed. The safe yielded $133, $17 worth of stamps, the money order and advance books plus the postal stamp.[2]

"Suspicious characters" had been observed in the vicinity the day of the burglary. They had, in fact, been helped across the Cimarron River by the sheriff. After the burglary was discovered, their movements were traced. The "suspicious characters" seemed to be traveling west, and law enforcement officers in that direction were notified. Their trail was picked up a few days later by a Deputy U.S. Marshall from Clayton, New Mexico. The men, known to be armed, had purchased horses along the way and led the posse on a long chase. The pursuit ended in a saloon in Antonochinco, Mexico, where they were arrested without incident after four men with Winchester rifles surrounded them. The prisoners had $20, $61 worth of stamps, and two incriminating drill bits in their possession. The men, who gave their names as William and Charles Pierce, brothers from Omaha, Nebraska, said they had purchased the stamps from a man in Nebraska and obtained the bits in a trade. Since only $17 worth of stamps had been stolen from the Ulysses post office, it was assumed they had "been in business for some time."[3]

They were extradited and returned to Kansas where the **Topeka Daily Capital** reported that they "never had a chance of escaping the penitentiary" although all the evidence against them was circumstantial. At their April 22, 1896 sentencing William Pierce, "the taller and older of the two," who had "the looks of a hardened criminal" asked Judge Foster if there was any doubt in his mind about their guilt.

Judge Foster replied, "There is not."

"You think we are guilty?" quizzed the defendant.

"I do."

"Then there is no use in beseeching your clemency?"

"There is no use."

"Well," replied the undaunted defendant, "I beseech it anyway."

Judge Foster was unmoved and pronounced the sentence. William and Charles Pierce were sentenced to five years at hard labor in the Leavenworth Penitentiary.[4] William Pierce was seventeen-year-old Jim McCloud. It was the first of many aliases that he would use during his lifetime. Leavenworth records indicate to this day that Jim McCloud was an alias of William Pierce's.[5] Only once, in Wyoming, did he use his true name prior to the death of his father.

A measles epidemic raged through Leavenworth in early May, 1897. Jim McCloud and another prisoner, both stricken so severely their heads were swollen, were quarantined in the prison hospital, away from the main prison population. They worked through the night of May 11 to loosen the bars over their sleeping room windows. At eight o'clock the next morning they crawled to freedom. Guards on horseback scoured the countryside, but prison officials held little hope for their recapture. It was believed that the damp, rainy day would be fatal to them. It may have been to McCloud's accomplice: no records can be located concerning him — even the fact that he was a prisoner cannot be verified. McCloud escaped with his life, but the escape eventually left him nearly blind.[6]

Nothing of his life from May, 1897 to September, 1898 can be learned. By September, 1898, he was living in Wyoming under the alias James Dale. During the night of September 3 the safe in the A. B. Daniels & Co. saloon at Douglas, Wyoming, was blown open by a technique not often seen by Wyoming lawmen. Two holes had been drilled into the safe. The first hole, drilled into the front, had been abandoned. The second, drilled into the top, had been filled with powder and fired.[7]

Two weeks after the safecrackers struck, **Bill Barlow's Budget** proclaimed that the arrest of the cracksmen "reads like a chapter from a nickel novel." Indeed it did. A local cowboy, twenty-five-year-old Edward Mewis, was the man Sheriff Joe Hazen suspected. Hazen and a deputy returned to Douglas and reported their "pursuit" of the safe-crackers ended near the infamous Hole-in-the-Wall. Sheriff Hazen then commissioned his prime suspect, Mewis, a deputy sheriff and dispatched him to Gillette under pretext. After the departure of Mewis, Hazen wired a legitimate deputy stationed in Gillette to watch Mewis when he arrived. Mewis, a compulsive gambler, deposited $200 in a bank then dropped $300 in a card game. Mewis paid his gambling debt with gold and was arrested. After Mewis' arrest a strange trans-formation occurred. Mewis the compulsive gambler became Mewis the compulsive talker. Telegrams bearing Dale's description, as fur-nished by Mewis, were sent to all area lawmen.[8]

A telegram was received in a few days from Natrona County Sheriff Rice. Rice informed Sheriff Hazen that he had James Dale in custody. Dale had $740 in his possession at the time of his arrest. Ironically, as an old man, Jim McCloud said that his maximum total past assets did not exceed $500. In Douglas, Mewis said that when the safe had blown open, he was sure "the entire building had caved in, and ran for the back door." According to Mewis, Dale never budged. Mewis said when he looked back, Dale was busy scooping the loot into a bucket before the smoke had cleared away. They divided the nearly $1,300 worth of money and gold near the Cheyenne River and parted.[9]

On September 27, 1898 Edward Mewis was sentenced to one year in the Wyoming penitentiary. James Dale, "who had had experience as a crook, and who did all the work" received a four year sentence.[10] Inside Jim McCloud's prison world, the January 7, 1902 transfer from the old penitentiary at Laramie to the new penitentiary at Rawlins was the most memorable occurrence. One imprisoned Jim McCloud never failed to earn the maximum amount of "good time" possible after his escape from Leavenworth. The only violation of prison rules noted on prison records was for "stealing food" during the 1930's at Leaven-worth. With 205 days "good time" to his credit, he was released March 5, 1902.[11]

After his release he remained in Wyoming, and became known around Buffalo and Thermopolis, where he lived, as "Driftwood

Jim" McCloud. His association with known criminals led him to be suspected of several crimes, but nothing could be proven. Among those crimes he was suspected of was the murder of sheepman Ben Minnick and the U.P. robbery. It was during the pursuit of the U.P. robbers that Sheriff Joe Hazen lost his life. McCloud numbered among his friends, Tom O'Day; Douglas horse thief George Pike, who once said that if he had a horse that he had come by honestly he would shoot it — before it contaminated the rest; and Earl Shobe, the man who killed Ben Minnick. It was because of this association that Johnson County Sheriff Dick Kennedy suspected "Driftwood Jim" after the safe in the Buffalo post office was blown open the night of April 27, 1903. Although safes in the Buffalo area had been "touched" before, the one at the Occidental Hotel within the past

week, it was the first time explosives had been used. Kennedy, who was not aware of "Driftwood Jim's" conviction as James Dale, launched an effort to find him. Sheriff Kennedy's investigation revealed that a hole was drilled into the top of the safe and filled with powder. The safe-crackers then wrapped wet bedding around the safe and fired the powder. Although the explosion blew the safe doors ten feet, the wet blankets had so effectively muffled the explosion few had heard anything.[12]

Jim McCloud, photographed after his conviction as James Dale. (*Photo: Courtesy Wyoming State Archives, Museums, and Historical Department.*)

In the meantime, a clue to the direction taken by the burglars came from the driver of the Kaycee mail stage. When the driver arrived in Buffalo he reported that he had found coins and powder scattered along the road, as if they had sifted from a torn receptacle. The coin and powder trail was followed until nightfall when a light snow obliterated all traces of it. The searchers made two significant discoveries: tracks indicated that a buggy had been held in waiting near

Trabing for the safecrackers, and the wire of an intentionally downed telephone pole on the Kaycee-Buffalo line had been snipped.[13]

The most plausible of several accounts concerning the arrest of "Driftwood Jim" McCloud was given by Edmo LeClair, the man who captured him. LeClair, affiliated with the Indian Police, and a companion returned to Thermopolis after having made a "general scout" of the area. When they returned, they spied Jim McCloud's horse hitched to the rail in front of Jack Hollywood's saloon. They circled around the saloon and entered through the back door. The smiling faces of McCloud's friends greeted them. McCloud had seen them ride past, retrieved his guns from back of the bar, and exited — unhampered through the front door. McCloud's friends poured out into the streets, loudly ridiculing the pair as they silently rode out of town. An ordinary man may have given up at this juncture, but LeClair was far from an ordinary man. They continued to ride until they were out of sight. They then doubled back to a place LeClair was certain McCloud would show up. They waited for him all night, and the next morning were rewarded by the sight of McCloud riding up the trail. When he was near them, LeClair called for him to surrender. McCloud dove from his horse and prepared to make his stand behind some boulders. LeClair's patience was equalled by his cunning. He was an old, very resourceful scout who knew all the tricks — even the old ones. LeClair and his companion propped up their hats — so they could be seen by McCloud — and circled around him. They were within twenty feet of him before he discovered them. The ruse drew the remark from McCloud, "I knew no tenderfoot was on the job."[14]

Tombstone of colorful Douglas horse thief George W. Pike. When McCloud was imprisoned as James Dale, he gave Pike's name as a personal friend in lieu of relatives. (*Photo: Courtesy American Heritage Center, University of Wyoming.*)

McCloud admitted to LeClair that he was very ill, and was taken to the Washakie Hotel in Thermopolis. After McCloud was securely chained to the bedpost in an upstairs room, a doctor was summoned. McCloud was too ill to escape on his own, but his many friends downstairs were all healthy. The night passed without an attempt to free him, but it was rumored that a gang, led by Tom O'Day, planned to liberate him at the first opportunity. The rumor became so prevelant

that sheriffs from the neighboring counties were called in when McCloud was transferred to Cheyenne. It proved to be a hoax, loose bar talk by the would-be rescuer who had another, much safer, plan: purjured testimony that would place McCloud far away from Buffalo the night of April 27. The transfer went without a hitch, and McCloud was safely landed in the Laramie County Jail in Cheyenne.[15]

Tom O'Day, one of the Belle Fourche bank robbers, and one of Jim McCloud's would-be rescuers. (*Photo: Author's collection.*)

In the Cheyenne jail at the time was one of the most controversial personalities of Western history: Tom Horn. Horn had been tried and found guilty of the murder of fourteen year old Willie Nickell. He was sentenced to hang. On August 9, McCloud called for the lone jailer, Richard Proctor, to bring him a glass of water. McCloud had feigned illness for several days prior to the request so Proctor unwittingly unlocked the door which opened into the jail corridor. Horn and McCloud rushed him. In the desperate struggle that ensued, Proctor was overpowered. After Horn and McCloud obtained Proctor's keys they pushed him into the sheriff's office. McCloud found a Winchester rifle in the sheriff's office, and put it to Proctor's head. Horn watched for anyone who might enter. When Proctor momentarily diverted McCloud's attention, he wrestled the Winchester away from McCloud. Proctor fired two shots before they were upon him again. Les Snow, another deputy, was standing outside the sheriff's office but didn't hear either shot. McCloud regained possession of the rifle. Proctor lunged for an automatic Belgian pistol, but Horn grabbed it. Deputy Snow entered the office and was covered by McCloud. Snow turned and ran, sounding the alarm that an escape was in progress. McCloud followed Snow out the door and ran to the jail livery. McCloud found the sheriff's horse and bolted down the street. Horn broke free from his struggle with Proctor and ran to the livery where he found that McCloud had taken the only horse. He ran from the livery, but was recaptured almost immediately by the operator of a merry-go-round. McCloud eluded capture longer, but didn't gain much more distance between himself and the jail than Horn did. After McCloud was observed peeking from the building in which he was hiding, he "threw up his hands" to a boy of twenty who covered him. Horn denounced Proctor and McCloud as he was taken back to jail. Horn said that if McCloud had not lost his nerve, both men could have escaped. That night a dozen special deputies were sworn in to guard the jail. The sheriff feared that an attempt to lynch Horn would be made, but no attack came.[16]

Richard Proctor's life went on. The intricate Julian scaffold took the life of Tom Horn November 3, 1903 as two of his friends sang "Life Is Like A Mountain Railroad." On November 13, 1903 Jim McCloud was indicted on two counts. Count one charged him with breaking and entering, while the second count charged him with the

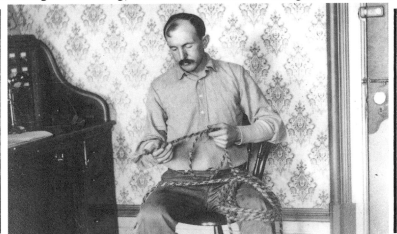

Tom Horn, Jim McCloud's cellmate, shown braiding a rope in the Cheyenne jail. Contrary to legend, Horn did not braid the rope with which he was hanged. (*Photo: Courtesy, Wyoming State Archives, Museums, and Historical Department.*)

theft of government property. It could not be proven which of his friends had assisted him; therefore, he was the only one indicted. Bond was set at $5,000 and he was remanded to jail in lieu of bond.17

Jailor Richard Proctor. (*Photo: Courtesy Wyoming State Archives, Museums, and Historical Department.*)

A confident Jim McCloud entered the courtroom, secure in the knowledge that he would soon be alibied to freedom. As in Kansas years earlier, though, he never had a chance of escaping the penitentiary. After four of the prosecution's witnesses testified that they had seen McCloud in Buffalo the night prior to the robbery his friends "weakened and threw up their hands." When the majority of the government's testimony was in McCloud changed his plea to guilty. On January 13, 1904 he was sentenced to four years in the penitentiary and fined $5. As McCloud was taken to the penitentiary another prisoner, who had received a longer sentence, remarked in sotto voice, "Lucky Jim, lucky Jim." Although it was known that he was an escapee from Leavenworth at the time of sentencing, he escaped the maximum sentence of five years and a $1,000 fine.18

Wyoming Penitentiary Inmate #802; Jim McCloud, photographed after his conviction for the Buffalo Post Office burglary. (*Photos: Courtesy, Warden Duane Schillinger, Wyoming State Penitentiary.*)

When he was received at the penitentiary an alert guard remembered him as former inmate James Dale.[19] Had it not been for the guard, McCloud's career as James Dale might never have been discovered. A comparison of the Wyoming Penitentiary records demonstrate the complexity of McCloud's frequent use of aliases:

IMPRISONED AS	JAMES DALE[20]	JIM McCLOUD[21]
Nativity:	Pennsylvania	Wyoming
Birth:	1870	1865
Occupation:	Stone Cutter	Carpenter

Upon McCloud's February 10, 1907 release, with 336 days "good time," a Leavenworth guard was in Rawlins to return him to Kansas. McCloud spent the first night en route to Kansas in the cell that he and Horn had occupied. The next morning before his departure McCloud told those who cared to listen that he meant to reform after his release. McCloud said that he had spent one-third of his life behind bars and was "getting tired of it." Philosophical about the life of an outlaw, McCloud said, "There's nothing to this life, and the glamour of the outlaw's life soon wears off when you get up against a stone pile."[22]

Near the expiration of his sentence, McCloud wrote a Wyoming friend that he hoped to return to Wyoming after his release and live an honest life. He was released July 12, 1912 but was never able to realize either dream. Alcohol, prohibition, and his admitted desire for easy money combined to return him to Leavenworth many times in the years ahead.[23]

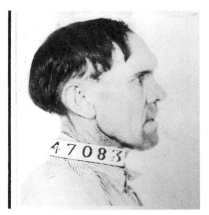 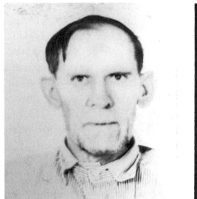

Jim McCloud, Leavenworth #47083, photograph taken in 1935. (*Photo: Author's Collection.*)

From prison records something of his life on the "outside" can be learned. He had worked as a farmhand, cotton picker, a short order cook, salesman, novelty salesman, and as a guard in a California winery. He married in 1921, and became a widower in 1926. It was also in 1926 that he was sentenced to prison for the first time for liquor law violations. He was sentenced to one year in Huntsville for "Manufacturing Liquor." In 1929 he obtained a license to marry again, but separated from his common law wife (records do not indicate that they were ever legally married) in 1937.[24]

The series of liquor law violations that would send him to prison many times had begun. In 1932 he served ninety days in the Federal jail in Chickasha, Oklahoma, for the sale and possession of liquor. McCloud was again sentenced to Leavenworth in 1935 for "Violation of Internal Revenue Laws." He was released March 20, 1936. In 1938 he was sentenced to Leavenworth for the same offense. Released on July 20, 1939 he was arrested six days after completing his conditional release period for "Sale of Liquor to Indians." It was the opinion of one prison official that "he has no desire to stay out of confinement as a result of the fact he is probably better cared for in this institution than he himself is able to out of confinement."[25]

After his 1941 release, it was three years before he was again sentenced to Leavenworth for what proved to be the last time. He was sentenced to five years for "Marihuana Tax Act and Sale of Liquor to Indians." When the sentence was handed down, McCloud remarked that it was "a pretty stiff sentence for an old man." He was sixty-four

years old at the time. He was
transferred to the Federal Correctional Institution on July 17,
1945. Although he was released
early (a court order reduced his
sentence), he had no visitors prior
to his June 4, 1946 release.[26]

Watt Carruth, Jim McCloud's last parole
advisor. A highly respected law enforcement officer, Carruth was also Jim Mc-
Cloud's friend. After a thirty year career
in law enforcement, Carruth served for
thirteen years as a baliff. *(Photo:
Courtesy, Mrs. Watt Carruth.)*

McCloud had operated a second-hand store in Anadarko,
Oklahoma, prior to his last sentence, and stated that he planned to
resume operating the store upon his release. At one o'clock the morning of December 15, 1954 Jim McCloud suffered a cerebral hem-
morage. Three hours later one of Wyoming's last long riders crossed
the divide.[27]

1.   Certificate of Death, James William McCloud, State of Oklahoma,
     Department of Health, Oklahoma City, Oklahoma; "Admission
     Summary," U.S. Penitentiary, Leavenworth, Kansas, (USPLK)
     1944; "Admission Summary, USPLK, 1939; "Preliminary Social Ab-
     stract," USPLK, undated.
2.   **Grant County** (Ulysses, Kansas) **Republican,** January 8, 1896.
3.   **Grant County Republican,** February 8, 1896.
4.   **Topeka** (Kansas) **Daily Capital,** April 23, 1896.
5.   Letter, D. L. Wilbourn, Manager Records Department, USPLK, to
     author, May 8, 1979.
6.   **Topeka Daily Capital,** May 14, 1897. Although the **Daily Capital**
     identified the other escapee as Oscar Sinley, two record searches
     (D. L. Wilbourn, Manager Records Department, May 27, 1981 and
     A. A. Padilla, Records Control Supervisor, June 17, 1981) failed to
     find a record for Sinley.
7.   **Bill Barlow's Budget** (Douglas, Wyoming), September 7, 1898.
8.   **Bill Barlow's Budget,** September 14 and 21, 1898.
9.   **Bill Barlow's Budget,** September 21, 1898.
10. Converse County (Wyoming) Court Records, State of Wyoming vs.
     James Dale, State of Wyoming vs. Edward Mewis, Douglas, Wyo-
     ming; "Description of Convict" Edward Mewis, Prison Records,
     Wyoming State Archives, Museums, and Historical Department
     (WSAMHD), Cheyenne, Wyoming.

11. Letter, Mrs. Ida Wozney, WSAMHD, to author, January 25, 1979; "Admission Summary", USPLK, 1944; "Convicts Discharged or Removed," Prison Record Books, WSAMHD, Cheyenne, Wyoming.

12. **Buffalo** (Wyoming) **Bulletin,** April 30, November 19, 1903; **Wyoming Derrick** (Casper, Wyoming), June 8, 1899; Tacetta B. Walker, **Stories of Early Days in Wyoming,** pp. 224-225.

13. **Buffalo Bulletin,** April 30, 1903.

14. Interview of Edmo LeClair by M. L. Simpson, June 22, 1926, typescript copy in American Heritage Center, University of Wyoming, Laramie, Wyoming.

15. Ibid.

16. **Buffalo Bulletin,** August 13, 1903.

17. Ibid., November 19, 1903.

18. Ibid., January 21, 1904.

19. Ibid., November, 1903. Although the article states John Dale, there was only one Dale ever sentenced to prison from Converse County, James Dale. Court records verify James Dale is correct. The article does not elaborate on how the guard was able to identify McCloud as former inmate James Dale before he was received at the penitentiary.

20. "Description of Convict" James Dale, Prison Record Books, WSAMHD, Cheyenne, Wyoming.

21. "Description of Convict" James McCloud, Prison Record Books, WSAMHD, Cheyenne, Wyoming.

22. "Convicts Discharged or Removed" James McCloud, Prison Record Books, WSAMHD, Cheyenne; **The Wyoming Tribune,** February 11, 1907.

23. **Cheyenne Daily Leader,** August 7, 1908; Letter, D. L. Wilbourn to author, May 8, 1979.

24. Letter, Billy D. Ware, Director of Classification and Records, Texas Department of Corrections, Huntsville, Texas, to author, July 17, 1979; "Admission Summary," USPLK, 1939; "Admission Summary," USPLK, 1944.

25. Letter, Wilbourn to author, May 8, 1979; "Admission Summary," USPLK, 1939; "Record of Court Commitment", Federal Correction Institution (FCI), Seagoville, Texas.

26. Letter, Wilbourn to author, May 8, 1979; "Admission Summary, USPLK, 1944; "Special Progress Report", FCI, August 2, 1945.

27. "Conditional Release Statement", FCI, May 29, 1946; Letter, Henry F. Hussey, Chief U.S. Probation Officer, Oklahoma City, Oklahoma, to author, July 18, 1979; Letter, Jeanette Prather, Smith Funeral Chapel, Anadarko, Oklahoma, to author, May 14, 1981.

NOTE: The records cited as USPLK and FCI, which I obtained photocopies of in 1979, were destroyed in 1980 during routine destruction of records after the elapse of thirty years.

DUNC BLACKBURN AND CLARK PELTON

Written and oral Blackburn family histories state that Duncan Ellis Blackburn, born January 25, 1848, "ran away to sea" while in his teens.[1] Contemporary Cheyenne and Deadwood newspapers indicate that the youthful Nova Scotia seaman: Became one of the most notable Black Hills road agents; contributed to the defeat of a sheriff, Seth Bullock, who failed to capture him, while the pursuit of the man who did, Scott Davis, became a Wyoming legend; and at the same time he remained well-liked, even by some who made his acquaintance "on the road."

A grand niece, Mrs. Gordon Maybee of Debert, Nova Scotia, provided an insight into the life of the young Duncan Blackburn: ". . . As Duncan was the eldest boy, it is probable that much of the farm work may have been his lot, and a life of such monotony, with absolutely no recreation must have been deadly. Sundays were days when nothing but the most necessary chores were done, and NO light reading . . . It is quite likely that these restrictions were, in fact, the reason for his leaving home . . . (His mother) was known even outside the family, as being a strict disciplinarian, and everyone stepped to her tune . . . by contrast, the father, Thomas E. Blackburn was reputed to be a kindly and rather gentle man, unable to cope with the iron will of his wife . . . as a family (they were) an extremely righteous and straight-laced outfit . . ."[2]

Blackburn may have remained "at sea" for a time because he did not arrive in the area he described as "west of the Missouri" until 1869. After his arrival in Cheyenne, Blackburn worked as a teamster for eighteen months, then went to Ft. Laramie and other posts where he held wood and hay contracts. In July, 1876, he returned to Cheyenne and made his departure for the Black Hills from there. He said that he became a horse trader in the Hills, with the business philosophy "whenever a man wanted to trade with me and I saw a chance to make something out of him, I traded." He further stated that after awhile, people "got down on him" and gave him a hard name, then the sheriffs and soldiers commenced chasing him, but he didn't know why.[3]

Cheyenne, Wyoming Territory, 1868. (*Photo: Courtesy Union Pacific Railroad Museum.*)

Actually, the why of the matter was quite simple, and a matter of record. By June of 1877, Blackburn had formed an unholy alliance with James Wall, Clark Pelton alias "Billy Webster" alias "The Kid," Robert "Reddy" McKimie alias "Little Reddy from Texas" and Bill Bevans. McKimie, the most dangerous of the five, had been ostracized from the Joel Collins-Sam Bass gang for the March 25 murder of Johnny Slaughter during a stage robbery.[4]

Hat Creek Station, c. 1883. (*Photo: Courtesy American Heritage Center, University of Wyoming.*)

According to McKimie, the above five of them were responsible for three robberies which occurred on consecutive days near the Cheyenne River late that June. The first robbery, the night of June 25th, netted them about $1,400 from the passengers. Although they "worked" on the treasure box for about an hour, they could not open it, nor could they break the rivets which secured it to the coach and haul it away.[5]

Hat Creek Station as it looks today. (*Photo: Courtesy Wyoming Travel Commission.*)

Inset of marker at Hat Creek Station. (*Photo: Courtesy American Heritage Center, University of Wyoming.*)

The second of the three robberies occurred the following night near the same place. Apprehensive because of the robbery the previous night, one of the two passengers rode beside driver Cy Hawley. Two miles from the Cheyenne River two armed men rose up from the ground and gave the command to halt. One of the passengers stuck his Spencer rifle out the window and fired at the road agents. At the same moment one of the robbers, called "Charlie" by his comrades, shot

Hawley in the side. The passenger had another bullet in the chamber of his gun, but a messenger warned him that they would probably all be killed if he fired again. "Charlie" was the recognized leader of the gang, and said it was "purely accidental" that Hawley had been shot. While two of the outlaws "went through" the passengers a third stood guard. The fourth went to work on the treasure box while "Charlie" oversaw the proceedings. The man who worked on the treasure box found that he could not open it and told Roberts, one of the messengers, that he knew Roberts had some powder and that he must give it up. The keyhole was filled with powder and blown, which caused fragments of the lock to fly about everyone's heads. The sacks and packages of gold dust from the treasure box were then thrown into an empty ore sack which several of the passengers were allowed to lift. Those who lifted the ore sack estimated that it weighed forty pounds. They then directed their attention to the treasure box from Custer. The wooden box was found to be empty and the road agents swore and threatened to "go over and burn Custer if treasure wasn't sent out from there soon." The value of the gold was estimated to be $12,800 by those who had been allowed to lift the ore sack. The passengers also contributed $1,200 to the "booty." Before they left the road agents gave Cy Hawley $20, and each of the passengers enough to pay their expenses to Cheyenne. Later McKimie admitted that he was "Charlie" and had shot Hawley.[6]

Later information revealed that five men had ridden past the Cold Spring Station, where the Deadwood and Custer roads joined, long before daylight the morning of the second robbery. It was assumed that they had been in Deadwood and obtained full information about the contents of the treasure box beforehand.[7]

The next night the stage was again stopped, but in a show of appreciation for the previous night's success, the passengers were not robbed, but bid "God speed." There was no messenger aboard the coach who conveniently carried powder and they were forced to saw off the part of the coach that the treasure box was attached to. They told the driver that, hereinafter, the treasure boxes must not be fastened down or locked so tightly, as it was hard work to break or blow them open and they were not working men, but "gentlemen of leisure." They also sent word by the driver to the managers of the stage line to send them a pair of gold scales, as "dividing dust with a spoon is not always satisfactory."[8]

After the third robbery they made their way, "with a disreputable woman," to South Pass City. When Pelton and McKimie were in

South Pass City purchasing supplies the woman overheard Bevans, Blackburn and Wall plotting to kill McKimie and Pelton. When Pelton and McKimie returned, she told McKimie of the plot, and with her aid, McKimie succeeded in getting the other members of the gang

too inebriated to realize what they were up to. McKimie and the woman then made off with $8,000 in gold dust and nearly $3,000 in greenbacks along with the best arms in camp. She and McKimie then made their way to the Point of Rocks station on the Union Pacific and traveled to St. Louis in style. When they arrived in St. Louis, McKimie said he gave the woman $1,000 and they parted.[9]

"Calamity Jane" left Hat Creek, "the home of our Robin Hoods," long enough in September of 1877 to get "drunker than a billed owl" in Deadwood. Hers was the first case of a woman being imprisoned in the Black Hills according to the **Black Hills Weekly Times,** September 23, 1877. (*Photo: Courtesy South Dakota Travel Commission.*)

Blackburn and Pelton soon returned to the Cheyenne River country and were seen at Ft. Laramie on July 21st. The following afternoon Deputy Sheriff Charles Hays learned that they were at the Six Mile Ranch, but planned to leave that night. Hays deputized the only men he could find, Adolph Cuny and a Mr. Sprague, and started for the Six Mile Ranch. When they arrived, Hays sent Cuny and Sprague to the front of the establishment, a combination bar, stage station, and "hog ranch." Cuny was instructed to enter through the front door and Sprague was to stand guard outside. Hays told them that he could go around and enter through the rear door. Hays entered from the kitchen and when he saw Cuny enter, he fully entered the bar portion of the establishment. One of the four men who were at a table engaged in a card game, was recognized by Hays as Dunc Blackburn.[10]

"Blackburn, I want you," Hays said.

"What for?" inquired Blackburn.

Hays didn't reply, and searched Blackburn. Blackburn was unarmed and Hays thought he recognized Pelton, but was unsure if it was he or not. Hays asked Bowman, the proprietor of the ranch, where the man who arrived with Blackburn was, and received the reply that Blackburn had arrived alone. Hays then "called upon him as a citizen of Wyoming" to help him find Pelton. Bowman then told Hays that Pelton was "outside somewhere." Hays told Cuny to watch them all, especially Blackburn, and he would go outside and search for Pelton. Prior to his departure he pointed out to Cuny the man he thought was Pelton, and told Cuny that if anyone moved, to kill him.[11]

Blackburn made a break for two guns that were behind the bar after Hays left. Cuny pointed his rifle at Blackburn and told him to sit down or he would "blow his brains out." Blackburn's actions diverted Cuny's attention long enough for the man Hays suspected of being Pelton to walk unnoticed into the dining room. Pelton then returned, and with Cuny's back to him, told Cuny to throw down his gun or he would kill him. Startled, Cuny turned towards him and Pelton fired. Cuny fired once in his direction, and Pelton fired the fatal shot.[12]

Hays, about one hundred yards away, heard the shots and ran back to the bar. The bar, with the exception of Cuny's body, was empty. Hays ran outside to see what direction Blackburn and Pelton took,

Laramie Hotel. The construction crews reached Laramie in June, 1868, and it soon became a thriving rail center with yard tracks and a combination dining hall and hotel, the large building in the center. *(Photo: Russell photo, Courtesy Union Pacific Railroad Museum.)*

but they were nowhere in sight. Hays was told they went in the direction of Deer Creek, but no one would assist him in an attempt to chase Blackburn and Pelton. Hays arrested Bowman and the other two men who had failed to identify Pelton and left Sprague in charge of them while he went to Ft. Laramie. Hays telegraphed Sheriff Carr in Cheyenne, then returned to the Six Mile Ranch with Capt. Lawson and twenty soldiers from Ft. Laramie, but Blackburn and Pelton had escaped.13

Laramie, Wyoming Territory, Freund's Gun Store, in 1868. *(Photo: A. C. Hull photo, Courtesy Union Pacific Railroad Museum.)*

Blackburn and Pelton were seen at a very early hour the morning of July 27th near Chase's ranch, twenty-five miles northwest of Cheyenne. Chase dispatched a courier to Cheyenne with a report of the sighting. Chase's description of the pair so accurately described Blackburn and Pelton that Sheriff T. Jeff Carr dispatched Deputy Sheriff Tom Talbot to the ranch. At Ft. Russell, Talbot was joined by Sergeant Major Gomey and four of the "best shots in Capt. Payne's company." No one needed to describe Blackburn to Talbot; he had attempted to arrest Blackburn the previous winter and Blackburn had drawn a gun on him. Talbot and the men traveled nearly all the way to Yellowstone Park, but could not cut the outlaw's trail, and returned.[14]

It was mid-August before Blackburn and Pelton were again recognized. About midnight the night of August 17th, Mr. Whitney, a well-known freighter over the Cheyenne-Deadwood route, was suddenly confronted by two men about a half-mile from his camp on Old Woman's Fork. One, who he recognized from his boyhood days as Dunc Blackburn, hollered, "Halloo, Frank, how are you?"

Dartmouth College graduate Henry Chase. Before his employment by the stage line, he had a ranch on Pole Creek, where Blackburn and Pelton were spotted. *(Photo: Courtesy Wyoming State Archives, Museums, and Historical Department.)*

After Whitney recovered from the shock of seeing two men who seemed to have arisen from the earth, the three entered into a friendly conversation. Blackburn told Whitney that he could prove he had been miles from the place when Johnny Slaughter was shot. In regard to the murder of Adolph Cuny, Blackburn again stated that he was innocent, a statement attested to by Pelton. "No, Blackburn didn't shoot Cuny;" Pelton said, "Here is the rifle that did it, and I am the man that fired it." They told Whitney that they had made a "big haul," but a companion named "Red" had made away with most of it.[15]

Robberies continued to be committed along the route, but it wasn't until the night of September 26th that Blackburn and Pelton were identified as the robbers. Messengers Scott Davis and James Denny were on the rear boot when the coach entered a shallow swale and the command to halt was heard. The command to halt was followed by two shots. Denny and Davis jumped to the ground. The yet unseen road agents then ordered everyone to throw down their arms and leave the coach. Two soldiers, the more frightened of the two with his hands over his head and screaming with fright, and another passenger ran from the coach. One of the soldiers knocked Davis' shotgun from his grip as he went by. Neither messenger had seen the robbers up to this time, but they soon caught sight of their heads in some tall grass. Davis had retrieved his shotgun and Denny fired the first of seventy shots they exchanged with the road agents

before the shell stuck in the breech of Davis' gun. Denny ran out of ammunition and Davis was shot in his left leg, just below the hip, as he reached for yet another rifle. The ball passed through his right leg and dropped into his boot. The messengers could make no more resistance and the three passengers returned to the coach with the cry, "We give up, we give up."

Scott Davis' pursuit of Blackburn and Wall resulted in the capture and arrest of two of the most notable Black Hills road agents. (*Photo: Courtesy South Dakota State Historical Society.*)

As the two road agents, who wore black masks and knew Davis by name, approached they announced that they had not come to do harm, but that they were merely on a "prospecting expedition." They gathered up the arms and said they had heard that a new safe had been put on the line, and that two messengers were being sent out with it. They thoroughly examined the safe, but made no attempt to open it. After they had satisfied their curiosity the outlaws complimented the messengers on their bravery and made their departure.

After their encounter with Davis and Denny, Blackburn and Pelton visited a hay camp on the Cheyenne River. Several of the men in the camp knew Blackburn and Pelton and advised them to leave the country at once. They said they planned to take the advice, but had not yet secured a "stake" and told them about the unfortunate episode they had with "Reddy."[17]

The stage company offered a one thousand dollar reward for the arrest and conviction of the two men who had been engaged in the skirmish with Davis and Denny, or two hundred dollars each for their bodies.[18] With such a tempting reward offered for them, they "laid low" until October 2nd, when they and two others stopped the Sidney coach near Buffalo Gap. The quartet was literally the Who's Who of Black Hills road agents: Dunc Blackburn, James Wall, Samuel Hartman alias "Laughing Sam," and Clark Pelton.[19]

Division Superintendent Ed Cook and a Mr. Ketchem from New York were the only occupants of the coach. The robbery netted only seven dollars cash, but when a demurrer was entered to the small amounts of funds the New Yorker carried, he tendered his note for an increased sum, after which the coach was allowed to pass.[20]

After the robbery new partnerships were formed which led to a great deal of confusion among contemporary newsmen and which has been passed down to later day historians. Blackburn, whose partner up to this time had been Clark Pelton, alias Billy Webster, alias "The Kid", was joined by James Wall, who was often confused in the press with Pelton. Blackburn and Wall, who was sometimes referred to as "The Kid" in his own right, continued to work the Cheyenne-Deadwood route. Pelton joined "Laughing Sam" and struck for Ft. Pierre. They were doomed; "Laughing Sam" and Pelton were soon arrested in Iowa for the theft of government property and horsetheft, respectively.[21]

1. Birthdate from Mrs. Blackburn's family Bible. This would have made Blackburn twenty-nine when he entered the Penitentiary and not thirty-two as he said he was. One written history that states he "ran away to sea" is The Tays Family Papers, Family Papers, Pans Manuscript Room, Public Archives of Nova Scotia, Halifax, Nova Scotia.
2. Mrs. Gordon (Phyllis) Maybee, R.R. 1, Debert, Nova Scotia, to author, June 25, 1980 and October 20, 1981. Mrs. Maybee also stated, ". . . as far as any of us knew, he had run away to sea at the age of seventeen."
3. **Cheyenne Daily Leader,** November 24, 1877. With the 1848 birthdate, there is an interval of four unexplained and unaccounted for years between when he left and when he arrived in the area described as "west of the Missouri."
4. **Cheyenne Daily Leader,** January 30, 1878, identified the gang as given. When Bevans was captured July 13, 1877, he had possession of a watch stolen from a passenger during the second robbery. In their visit with Mr. Whitney, Blackburn said they had made a big haul, but a companion named "Red" got away with most of it; a story he repeated at the hay camp on the Cheyenne River. Robert McKimmie's account, found in J. W. Bridwell's **Life and Adventures of Robert McKimie,** p. 8, tallies with the **Leader's** identification and gives "Reddy's" account of how it was accomplished.

5. **Cheyenne Daily Leader,** June 28, 1877.
6. **Cheyenne Daily Leader,** June 29, 1877; **Black Hills Weekly Pioneer,** June 30, 1877. Later "Reddy" admitted that he was "Charlie" and it was he who shot Hawley.
7. **Cheyenne Daily Leader,** June 29, 1877.
8. **Cheyenne Daily Leader,** June 29, 1877; **Black Hills Daily Times,** June 28, 1877.
9. J. W. Bridwell, **Life and Adventures of Robert McKimie,** p. 8. Blackburn's statements add substance to McKimie's account of how it happened that Blackburn and Pelton hadn't made a "stake." "Calamity Jane" was known to be around Hat Creek at this time, and claimed to have been the source of McKimie's information. That she was in the area is fact; her claim, however, was not made until after Bridwell's book was published.
10. **Cheyenne Daily Sun,** May 28, 1879, published a letter from Hays to Carr, dated July 23, 1877. The movements of those who remained inside while Hays went outside is a composite of the stories he received from those who remained.
11. Ibid.
12. Ibid.; **Cheyenne Daily Leader,** July 25, 1877. Cuny's funeral took place July 23, 1877 and he was buried in the citizens graveyard adjoining the military cemetery at Ft. Laramie. "Thus has passed away at the age of 42 years, one of the oldest pioneers of this territory"; **Cheyenne Daily Leader,** July 26, 1877.
13. **Cheyenne Daily Sun,** May 28, 1879.
14. **Cheyenne Daily Leader,** July 28, 1877.
15. **Cheyenne Daily Leader,** August 22, 1877; **Black Hills Daily Times,** August 20, 1877.
16. **Black Hills Daily Times,** September 29, 1877; **Cheyenne Daily Leader,** September 29, 1877.
17. **Cheyenne Daily Leader,** November 16, 1877. The report states this occurred "just after" their encounter with Davis and Denny. It is probable that the delay in the reporting of their visit to the camp was due to slow transportation, or it is possible that this was the date one of the men in the camp made the first trip to Cheyenne since they had been there.
18. **Cheyenne Daily Leader,** November 22, 1877. The reward notice that appeared in the **Leader** was under date of September 27, 1877.
19. **Black Hills Daily Times,** October 4, 1877; **Cheyenne Daily Leader,** October 4, 1877. The **Leader** was the only one of the two that identified the robbers, but the participants named tallies with Blackburn's statement that he and Pelton split up, and the fact that Pelton and "Laughing Sam" were arrested together in Iowa.
20. Ibid.
21. Less than a week later Pelton was arrested in Iowa by a deputy U.S. Marshal.

DUNC BLACKBURN &
JAMES WALL

A week later, on October 9th, Blackburn and Wall stopped the "up" (Deadwood bound) coach. Jack Bowman, the proprietor of the Hat Creek stage station, and no relation to the Bowman at Six Mile, was a passenger. Bowman, upon his arrival in Deadwood told a reporter:

There were only four of us passengers — a lady and her two children who occupied a seat inside, and myself. I was on the box with George Chapman, the driver, and we were booming along at a pretty good pace when we heard the command to halt. The night was dark and we could see no one. George didn't pull up quick enough, and we heard the gun locks click. I at once recognized the voice of Blackburn, as he used to work for me, so I replied, "Oh, no, you don't want me to get down." They came up to the coach, and inquired who in ----- I was, and ordered me to get down. I laughed at Dunc and he recognized me. They pulled off their masks, and passed up a flask of whiskey, and then wanted to know if there was anyone inside, and when I said "no," but that I had some. They replied, "O, ----, we don't want your money." Dunc asked me what was being said in town about the frequent robberies, and who was getting credit for it, and when I replied they were, Dunc said, "O, I suppose so." I told them that soldiers were on the road, which made them both laugh and drew from Wall the remark, "I wish they would put a company of cavalry on our trail, we could make some money out of their horses." I asked Dunc if they were mixed up in

the Homan robbery and he said no, although he knew he had
the credit of it. Turning to the driver he said, "Well, George,
I will never ask you to put the brakes on again, we are going
to quit the road; business is too ------ bad."[1]

A few days after their chat with Bowman a ranchman reported at
Crook City that he had seen, and ridden some distance with Wall. A
posse from Crook City started up the Bismarck road in pursuit. Soon
they saw the Bismarck coach motionless, with two mounted men by its
side, apparently in conversation with the passengers. The horsemen
observed the approach of the Crook City men and quickly fled. Blackburn and Wall were within a mile of Crook City before they were able
to elude their pursuers. After the coach arrived in Crook City it was
found Mr. Gidley, the superintendent of the line, was the only occu-
pant.[2]

Towards evening Sheriff Seth Bullock and some of his deputies
secreted themselves near Crook City. About midnight two men were
seen riding into town from the
lower end. Bullock ordered them
to halt at the same time one of his
deputies accidentally fired a shot.
The outlaws, alarmed, turned
their mounts around and galloped back down the street. As they
fled, Bullock's party fired random shots at them. A search of
the area revealed a large amount
of blood, and it was presumed
that one of the outlaws had been
hit.[3]

Seth Bullock (*Photo: Courtesy South
Dakota State Historical Society.*)

The next day it was learned that Blackburn had sustained two
shots in his arm and had received food and medical aid at a nearby
ranch. At the ranch, Blackburn vowed that he would kill Bullock in
twenty-four hours. It proved to be an empty threat, for Blackburn and
Wall were forced to make a hard ride for the Cheyenne River with a
posse hot on their trail.[4]

Although Blackburn and Wall had committed no crimes in Lawrence County, Bullock's inability to capture Blackburn and Wall, and

other road agents, became one of the major issues in his re-election campaign. When the votes were tabulated, Bullock had been defeated by Johnny Manning in a close race. Although he was later appointed U.S. Marshal by three presidents, Seth Bullock was a one term sheriff in Lawrence County and that was by appointment.[5]

Blackburn kept his word to George Chapman; it was the last stage he was known to have stopped. The light at the end of the tunnel was the dawn of a new era, and Blackburn recognized it for what it was.

On the night of November 10th, Blackburn and Wall stole seventeen head of horses from the Lance Creek stage station. Scott Davis

had recovered from the wounds he sustained on the night of September 26th, and telegraphed Luke Voorhees for authority to go after the thieves. Authority was granted and Davis began his pursuit; a pursuit that became a legend.[6]

Luke Voorhees, Superintendent and part owner of the Cheyenne and Black Hills Stage and Express Company. Voorhees was the territorial treasurer and later elected receiver of public monies and disbursing agent of the U.S. land office in Cheyenne. (*Photo: Courtesy American Heritage Center, University of Wyoming.*)

Davis left Ft. Laramie with four men and a non-commissioned officer from Ft. Laramie. Davis soon cut a trail west of Ft. Laramie that he believed to be the trail of the thieves. Davis and the men followed the trail to Ft. Fetterman, then on to Ft. Caspar, and continued to follow the Oregon Trail to Independence Rock, through Devil's Gate, and into the Sweetwater Valley. The soldiers mutinied; their horses were jaded and a heavy snow had fallen. Alone, Davis pressed on to Camp Stambaugh where he was compelled to stop and rest. His own horses were worn out; he was exhausted and famished. Rest, then onward, to South Pass City, then by stage to Green River.[7]

DAVIS' ROUTE IN PURSUIT OF
BLACKBURN AND WALL

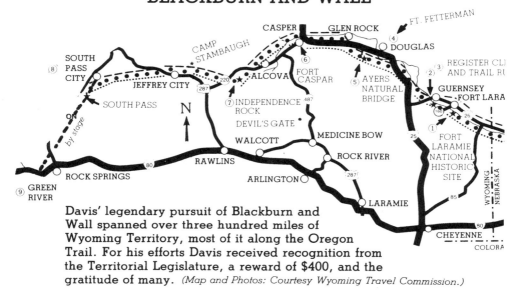

Davis' legendary pursuit of Blackburn and
Wall spanned over three hundred miles of
Wyoming Territory, most of it along the Oregon
Trail. For his efforts Davis received recognition from
the Territorial Legislature, a reward of $400, and the
gratitude of many. *(Map and Photos: Courtesy Wyoming Travel Commission.)*

1. Scott Davis left Ft. Laramie on November 19, 1877. Ft. Laramie, bought by the Government from fur traders for $4,000 in 1849, was a major military post along the Oregon Trail. Many of the buildings have been restored and it was made a National Historic Site in 1960.

2. Register Cliff, a major campsite along the Oregon Trail, rises one hundred feet above the prairie. On its face are carved the names and hometowns of many who passed by it during the 1850's and 1860's.

3. The Oregon Trail ruts and footpaths of the bullwhackers who walked along beside the teams are still highly visible. Now a National Historic Landmark.

4. Sign marking the site of the Fetterman Massacre. Fort Fetterman was named for Lieutenant Colonel William J. Fetterman. *(Photo: Courtesy Wyoming Travel Commission.)*

5. Ayers Natural Bridge, slightly off the Oregon Trail, a major landmark on the Oregon Trail. The bridge measures twenty feet high and ninety feet across.

6. Fort Caspar, 1858-1867, has also been restored and many of the buildings are open to the public. A museum is housed in one of the buildings.

7. Independence Rock, "The Great Register of the Desert", covers twenty acres at its base, with a three or four acre area on top. More than 50,000 names were carved on "the Register."

8. South Pass City, the boom town of 4,000 in 1869, is where Davis boarded the stage to Green River. He had been in the saddle for eight days.

9. Davis arrived in Green River nine days after leaving Ft. Laramie, and one day after he lost Blackburn and Wall's trail.

A dejected Davis arrived in Green River the evening of November 19th, nine days after he had left Ft. Laramie. He had followed the thieves over three hundred miles — then lost their trail. Two hours after he arrived in Green River a telegram from Sandy Station was received with the information that a party trailing horses had recently passed there.

About nine o'clock that night Davis, accompanied by Charles Brown and Charles "Pawnee Charlie" Gorsuch, was back in the saddle and on a good scent. After a hard, four hour ride, they arrived at the Alkali stage station and awoke "Bronco Jim," the man in charge. Jim's loud, excited voice in turn woke up Blackburn and Wall, who were asleep in a nearby haystack. "Pawnee Charlie" saw the pair as they attempted to run from their hiding place and called for them to halt. Neither stopped and Davis, Brown, and "Pawnee Charlie" fired simultaneously. One of the men fell. Davis and his assistants searched for the horses, but only found one, and returned to the man they had wounded. Wall gave his name as "Thomas Woodby" and begged for his life. Wounded in both legs he told his captors, "You boys have put a pair of shackles on me that I can't get off."

Wall told them that in his hurry, Blackburn had left behind his hat, boots, and coat. He did have a gun, but only two bullets for it; one in the chamber and the other in his pocket. Wall said Blackburn had about $200 with him, but it was consensus of the group that Blackburn "could not survive long, unless helped by someone."[8]

After Brown had left on the stage with Wall in his custody, Davis and "Pawnee Charlie" searched the haystack and found a revolver which had been taken from Davis during an earlier robbery. They also found the horses and returned to Green River with them.[9]

About eight o'clock the next night a man, suspiciously without a hat or coat and his feet wrapped in underwear, entered Barrett's Store in Green River. He purchased a new hat, coat, boots and overshoes, then made his way to Pete Appel's restaurant. Davis and his assistants were informed of the man's arrival and began "keeping cases" on him. "Pawnee Charlie" and another man were deputized to make an arrest. They entered Appel's and told Blackburn that he was wanted. Blackburn replied, "All right, but if I had my gun I would stand you off." He admitted that he was Blackburn and a search revealed that he was unarmed, but had three buckskin pouches, some old coins, a pen knife, $150, and a watch. He then showed the man where his revolver was hidden and made a present of it to "Pawnee Charlie."

He was placed in the Green River jail with Wall until transportation to Cheyenne could be arranged.[10]

Blackburn and Wall were returned to Cheyenne under strong guard. A delegation of lawmen and curious onlookers met Davis and his prisoners at the depot, from where they were quickly escorted to jail. Blackburn sported the latest innovation in shackles; a new, more effective version of the ball and chain. Blackburn was taken into Sheriff Carr's office and Wall, to the pleasure of an eager, gaping crowd, was left on a crude stretcher in the hallway.[11]

After the lawmen interviewed Blackburn, both men were placed in the jail proper. Blackburn recognized several of the prisoners who had recently been brought to Cheyenne from Deadwood. He also recognized Tom Mulqueen, who had been one rated by Wyatt Earp as one of the top men with a gun in Deadwood in '76. Blackburn reminded Mulqueen that he and Blackburn had once traveled to the Hills together.[12]

During an interview with a **Cheyenne Daily Leader** reporter, Blackburn said that after Pelton had shot Cuny, they traveled to Laramie City. Pelton refused to enter the town, but that he himself had made several trips in for supplies. On his first trip into town he read a newspaper that was laying on the counter of a store and learned that Talbot and a squad of cavalrymen were hot on their trail. On his second trip to Laramie City he again read the newspaper, and found that Talbot and his men were only a few miles away. Blackburn said he immediately returned to their camp on Rock Creek and he and Pelton started for Ft. Pierre. Before they reached Pierre, however, Pelton left him and he was joined by Wall.[13]

On Saturday, December 8, 1877, Blackburn was arraigned upon four indictments — one for obstructing the United States mail, one for highway robbery, one of assault with intent to murder, and one for grand larceny. For the indictment for robbery, he was sentenced to three years in the penitentiary; for grand larceny, two years; for assault to murder, three years; and on the charge of obstructing the United States mail, a fine of ninety-nine dollars was levied.[14]

James Wall was arraigned upon the same charges and received identical prison sentences and a ninety-nine dollar fine. Both men were remanded to the Laramie County jail to await transfer to the Territorial Penitentiary.[15]

About five o'clock the evening of December 16th, the regular suppertime for Sheriff Carr's fourteen "birds," a situation developed which caused Carr to exclaim the next day, "I'm a lucky fellow; darned if I ain't." Carr had opened the door and swung it open wide enough to allow "Old Fritz" Freemong and the cook to carry in the prisoners' meals. Four of the 'birds', Blackburn, Baker, Williams, and Collins were standing by the door. Carr glanced at them, then at something near the stove which caught his attention. The four sprang on him, hissing, "You son of a bitch, we've got you now." Carr reached for the revolver he carried in his pocket and felt it fall to the floor. Williams obtained possession of the gun and was encouraged by the other three to shoot Carr. Carr had rehearsed "Old Fritz" many times about what to do in an emergency situation, and yelled for help. Unfortunately, the rehearsals did not include the actual fright "Old Fritz" and the cook were experiencing at that moment. Baker exited the cell, followed by Williams, who met "Old Fritz" in the kitchen and pointed the revolver at him.[16]

In the cell, with only Blackburn and Collins, Carr managed to free the grip of the man who held his arm and knocked Collins down. Just at that moment another prisoner, who had been working in the kitchen, ran into the cell and gave Carr a revolver. Carr fired at Collins and missed, but the revolt ended, "Every one of the prisoners seeking the bottom of the pile of blankets in his cell."[17] A count was taken and it was discovered that Collins had returned to his cell during the melee. Williams, the only missing prisoner, was soon discovered in an old house not far from the jail and returned to his cell.[18]

Blackburn was again safely behind bars when Pat, an Irishman who guarded the snowshed between Laramie and Cheyenne, visited Cheyenne. Pat was in a bar, and in a reflective mood when he recalled the only time he had met "Doonk" Blackburn:

"Doonk Blackburn rid up to me, hild a pistol at me oye, an' tould me to throw up me hands. All right, says I, I'll do it, but fhere the divil will I throw 'em to? 'Throw 'em up' says he, an' up they wint. Thin he wint through me pockets, an' tuk a hundred an' eighty dollars that I had saved up. He wint to me cabin and tuk me grub an' blankets an' rid off. Bad cess to him."

The experience convinced the usually thrifty Irishman that it was no use to save his money; that it would be better spent for whiskey. Pat bought a round for the house, walked over to the bar and reasoned out loud, "If ye save it an' sind it home a thavin' mail clerk will stale it; if ye lind it to the brakemen they'll niver think o' payin' a cint of it back; if ye put it in the bank the domd bank'll bust, and if ye kape it in yere pocket some divilish shpalpeen loike Doonk Blackburn will be afther puttin' a pistol in yere oye an' tillin' yes to throw up yere hands."[19]

Duncan Ellis Blackburn and James Wall were transported to prison in a special car provided by the railroad. They began serving their sentences Christmas Day, 1877.[20]

1. Jack Bowman, the proprietor of the Hat Creek stage station, was later Sheriff of Gunnison County, Colorado. Bowman later married Sarah Smith, the ex-wife of D. Tom Smith, the woman he employed at Hat Creek as a housekeeper.

2. **Black Hills Daily Times,** October 20, 1877. **The Cheyenne Sun,** December 9, 1877 used this conversation between the outlaws and Mr. Gidley to suggest a "dastardly conspiracy" that it supposed existed between the outlaws and the Bismarck line, in which they were paid to leave the Bismarck coaches alone.

3. Ibid.

4. Ibid.; **Black Hills Daily Times,** October 25, 1877. **The Black Hills Daily Times** article seems to be far more objective than any article either it or **The Miner,** which supported Johnny Manning, had printed up to this time.

5. **Black Hills Daily Times,** October 25, 1877. **The Times** erred in its statement that Blackburn and Wall had not committed any crime in Dakota Territory. The October 2, 1877, robbery was near Buffalo Gap.

6. **Cheyenne Daily Leader,** November 22, 1877; Agnes Wright Spring, **The Cheyenne and Black Hills Stage and Express Routes,** pp. 234-239.

7. Spring, op. cit.; **Cheyenne Daily Leader,** op. cit.

8. **Cheyenne Daily Leader,** November 23, 1877.

9. Ibid.; **Black Hills Daily Times,** November 21, 1877.

10. Ibid.

11. **Cheyenne Daily Leader,** November 24, 1877.

12. Ibid.

13. Ibid.

14. **Cheyenne Daily Leader,** December 9, 1877.

15. Ibid.

16. **Cheyenne Daily Leader,** December 15, 1877.

17. Ibid.; **Annals of Wyoming,** Vol. 20, No. 2, pp. 174-175.

18. Ibid.

19. **Cheyenne Daily Leader,** January 1, 1878.

20. **Cheyenne Daily Leader,** December 26, 1877.

"LITTLE BROCKY'S" LAST RAID

Had a cowboy not found the skull of a white man on Horsehead Creek[1] in 1881, "Little Brocky's" last raid would probably not have been remembered.[2] "Lame Johnny," contemplating a horse stealing raid on the Whetstone and Cheyenne River Agencies, selected "Tony Pastor" and "Little Brocky" to accompany him. A fourth man, along for the excitement only, also made the horse gobbling expedition.

Through the writings of E. T. "Doc" Peirce, let us now digress back to March, 1878, and accompany the quartet on this, "Little Brocky's" last raid.

They started out in great spirits but had a pretty hard trip of it. They rounded up sixty-eight head of stock and got started by three o'clock one morning, but the Indians missing their horses gave chase, and just as the sun was rising the boys could see them coming over a hill not more than a mile behind them. They soon overtook the white men and shooting began from both parties, but the boys kept the herd moving along.

Johnny killed one Indian and crippled another. Pastor killed one and Brocky was shot through the arm and wanted to give up, but Johnny would not stand any foolishness. He ordered the visitor to take the lead and gave him a sight to ride for, and told Pastor to keep the ponies running. He next tied Brocky into the saddle and turned his horse into the herd so they would be sure to keep along and not fall into the hands of the Indians.

After looking after these details, Johnny formed himself into a rear guard and whenever he came over a hill he would stop and wait until the Indians came in range and then open his battery, thus giving the boys a chance to get along with the stock. Some of the horses were killed or crippled by the long range guns. After a running fight of many miles, the storm overtook them; a genuine blizzard. The Indians gave up the chase, but the boys kept traveling toward the Hills.

Bear Butte. (*Author's Photo.*)

The air was so full of snow they could not see Bear Butte or Harney Peak and they soon were lost. They had lost or thrown away their clothing in the fight and were freezing. Brocky begged to be shot, and Pastor wanted to comply with his request, but Johnny would not listen to it, but gave the wounded, freezing boy a terrible thrashing with his quirt thinking in that manner to get him mad and so take fresh courage.

Mt. Harney. (*Photo: Courtesy South Dakota Division of Tourism.*)

It was no use. Brocky begged to die, so Johnny stopped the caravan and roped the best horse in the outfit, saddled it, and tied it to the sage brush and laid Brocky down in the snow beside it, saying perhaps he will get frightened after we have gone and get up and follow us. By this time the ravines were drifted full and it took hard work to get the floundering horses through them.

They finally reached the Cheyenne, at the mouth of Battle River, a place afterwards made famous by Col. Day and his troops in the Messiah War. There they camped while Johnny rode to the stage station and got clothes and food. Only thirteen head of horses remained to be brought to the Hills.

Tony Pastor was hanged on the Denver Road a short time after. Brocky was never heard from again, but in 1881 a cowboy brought a white man's skull into Rapid City, which he had found precisely the place where Johnny said they had left Brocky, so there was nothing left to do but write "Brocky" across that empty forehead and place it upon the mantle piece for ornamental purposes.[3]

After the storm subsided "Lame Johnny" returned to look for the body of his friend, but was unable to find the place they had left him.[4] One wonders how many other young men like "Little Brocky," their aliases known only to their outlaw associates, their true names known only to God, faced death in the Black Hills, frightened and so very, very alone.

1.   Named Horsehead Creek by General Custer during his 1874 expedition, it has been renamed and can be found on the present day maps as Cottonwood Creek in Fall River County. Virginia Driving Hawk Sneve, ed., **South Dakota Geographic Names**, pp. 176 and 201.
2.   **Black Hills Journal,** September 24, 1881.
3.   Ellis Taylor Peirce, "Odd Characters and Incidents in the Black Hills During the 70's."
4.   **Black Hills Journal,** op. cit.

"PERSIMMON BILL"

Jim Abney's stable on Sixteenth Street was the gathering place for Cheyenne's old frontier gossips. It was 1879, and the west as they had known it was disappearing. Nick Janise made the statement that "Persimmon Bill's dead," and questionable as his remark was, Janise held the floor. They allowed one another a little literary license, and believed that what really happened shouldn't interfere with a good story. After Janise finished his narrative, a young man, employed in one of Cheyenne's hotels, remarked, "I knew Persimmon Bill well."

"You did?" said Abney, Janise, and others in chorus.

"Yes, I did; and I possess the history of that noted outlaw's life as told to me individually when Bill took me and my outfit in on Injun Creek in the spring of seventy-six. If you will square 'round I will tell you boys how it was."

Of course, they all squared around, and the young man liked to have set a record for uninterrupted tongue waggin' at Abney's. Nary a one of those old gossips interrupted, and we shan't either:

There was four of us in our party. Me,[1] D. Tom Smith and Charley Potter, both from Denver, and a Union Pacific conductor named Murphy. We were on our way from Custer to Cheyenne in March seventy-six. While driving leisurely along over the desolate expanse of alkaline badlands, just south of the Cheyenne River, our little party ran into a party of Sioux Indians, among whom a pleasant-featured, well dressed white man was noticed. After the first fright occasioned by the sudden meeting with the large body of Indians had somewhat subsided, I addressed the white man and, like a fool, asked him what he was doing with the Indians — they were Ogalalas on their way to the Red Cloud Agency. The stranger's little blue eyes twinkled with fun, and he laughed loudly at the question. Then turning to the Indians, who look-ed silently on while our two wagons were being emptied by the squaws, repeated the reporter's question. Then the Indians laughed, and to be polite we tried to do likewise, but with poor success, for we were badly scared. "No," said the white stranger, "I am Persimmon Bill; some call me Sogerkilling Bill, while those who desire to be polite call me Government William." Our party did not desire to hear anymore. If we had been miserable before, the announced presence of this notorious cutthroat and outlaw did not contribute to our hap-piness. There is an old saying that, "The devil is not so bad as he is painted," and certainly Persimmon Bill, with all his bloody crimes upon his hands, was not a bad man to look upon; and above all he has a great respect for gentlemen of the press, which he afterwards made apparent by his actions.

After our arrival in the Indian camp, to which we were escorted by some eighteen or twenty braves, Persimmon Bill welcomed me to his little fire, which was separate from the In-dian's fire, and bade me make myself comfortable, as no harm was intended toward me or my companions; that the In-dians were friendly and had been sent to the agencies by the Crook Expedition, then in the Big Horn Mountains.[2] The outlaw was soon afterwards stretched upon his buffalo robe undergoing a systematic interviewing ordeal. The story of his life is brief and rather commonplace. He said he was born in the little village of Murphysville, Cherokee County, in the mountains of North Carolina.[3] The war broke out when he was about sixteen years old, and he, with his two brothers, en-listed in the Twenty-third North Carolina regiment.[4] He deserted the Confederate army and joined Burbank's Union Kentucky Cavalry,[5] but in a fight with a comrade about a woman, while at Bowling Green,[6] he drew a pistol and shot him. He made his escape to Morgan's command and was soon afterwards captured while on a raid into Ohio, and was sent to Johnson's Island,[7] where he remained until near the close of the war.

Early in 1867, Chambers made his way to Cheyenne, where he became associated with a crowd of roughs, who, just prior to the completion of the Union Pacific to Cheyenne, made this region anything but a pleasant resort.[8] Here he fell into the hands of the outraged people, who hung two or three of his "pals," and spared his life on the condition that he left town at once.[9] He went to Fort Collins, where he succeeded in stealing a horse and made his escape to North Platte, where he was allowed only a short time to remain. Up to the year 1870 he said he had kept pretty sober, and had never murdered a man for money or spite. About the close of this year he found himself at Sioux City, with about four hundred dollars in money and a good horse. While in a drunken frenzy he shot his horse on the street. The brother of the sheriff, who was acting as deputy sheriff of Woodbury County,[10] attempted to arrest Bill, who shot him through the arm. He was arrested and ironed, but succeeded in working his way out of jail. He induced a man to chop the chain connecting his manacles, and thus made his way to the hotel, where he procured a pistol, and then started out for more drink and a row.

Observing a half-breed (who afterwards became his companion) named Jules Semino,[11] riding a fine horse down the street, he inquired the price of it. "Ninety dollars," said the half-breed. "It's mine," said Bill, "get off, I want to try it."

After riding up and down the street a few times he returned to the hotel, where he was met by the sheriff, who ordered him to surrender. Bill requested that he unlock his "bracelets." The sheriff, supposing that his unruly prisoner intended to go along without trouble, unlocked the broken handcuffs when Bill immediately shot him down,[12] and after smashing out the office windows, ran downstairs, mounted the half-breed's horse and dashed away and escaped.

A reward of $1,000 was offered for his apprehension, but he was never arrested.

After filling and relighting his pipe, which he handed to me to try, Bill continued his story. He said he knew that he would swing if taken, and made all haste out to the mountains, and located in South Pass City. But business being dull there, he went to Sherman, on the line of the Union Pacific,[13] where, in company with two or three others, he became a "road agent" or robber. Said he, "We just took whatever we thought would sell in Laramie City or Cheyenne, but we never robbed poor men." At last Bill, in one of his drunken sprees,

gutted and robbed the livery stable at Sherman, and, taking
the best stock, started across to the Sweetwater Mountains,
where he joined the Indians, with whom he had been carrying
on a trade in horseflesh and arms ever since.

Sherman Windmill & Station, 35 miles west of Cheyenne, 1870. *(Photo: Courtesy Union Pacific Railroad Museum.)*

On the 6th of March, 1876, two or three days after
General Crook's Big Horn Expedition marched away from
Fort Fetterman,[14] Persimmon Bill walked boldly into the
Sutler's store at that post. He says he knew there was no
cavalry in the post, and that no one would be looking for him,
as no one in the garrison knew him personally, except the
squaws and half-breeds, and they would not "give him
away." He called the three infantry officers who were playing
billiards to "come take a drink." Major Chambers, of the
Fourth Infantry,[15] who was in command of the post, declined, in a haughty tone, the imperious call of the outlaw.
Bill then called upon one or two enlisted men to drink. They
drew back in alarm, when Bill, in a rage, drew a revolver, and

Sherman Station, Wyoming Territory, "The highest railway station in the world." *(Photo: Courtesy Wyoming State Archives, Museums, and Historical Department.)*

announcing his name to the now thoroughly indignant officers, who were unarmed, ordered them out of the room, while he, after pocketing a bottle of whiskey and some cigars, mounted his horse and dashed out of the post just as the "long roll" was waking up the little garrison. Piqued at his reception in Fetterman, and half frenzied with whiskey, he rode along towards Jack Hunton's ranch, where he suddenly came face-to-face with Sergeant Sullivan, of Company F, Fourth United States Infantry. He rode past a short distance, "and then," said this cold-blooded murderer, "I remember seeing that sergeant have some money at Owen's ranch a few days before, so I just turned 'round and plugged him in the back. The sergeant fell from the horse he was riding, which galloped on towards the fort." The murderer took about $300 and a gold watch from the victim, and also carried off his nee-

dle gun and ammunition.[16] He laughed merrily while he recited this last murder, and closed by saying: "I am death on soldiers and government property, and that's why they call me Government Bill."

Major General George Crook, born at Dayton, Ohio, September 23, 1829; graduated from West Point, class of 1852; died, Chicago, Illinois, March 21, 1890. When Red Cloud learned of the death of "the Grey Fox," he said, "Then General Crook came; he, at least never lied to us. His words gave the people hope. He died. Their hope died again. Despair came again." (*Photo: Courtesy Wyoming State Archives, Museums, and Historical Department.*)

The continued outrages, horse stealing and robbery committed by "Bill" and his gang prompted the government to offer a reward of $1,000 in addition to the $1,000 offered in Sioux City for the arrest of "Persimmon Bill." Gen. Bradley, the post commander at Fort Laramie, offered the reward with the significant words added, "dead or alive."

Few wanted to take the contract of taking him at that time, as his name was a terror on the Cheyenne and Black Hills road.

With our narrator firmly entrenched in the annals of Abney's stable for uninterrupted jawboning, one of his captive audience asked the question, "How did he look?". Here we shall pause to clarify the killing of Sergeant Sullivan, and add some additional information.

"Persimmon Bill" had been a "compulsory boarder at the Hotel d'O'Brieno" in March, 1875, for "hovering occasionally on the outskirts of the Indian horse herd near Red Cloud."[17] Apparently he windbagged his way through a grand jury, for he turned up again before the year was out. Late in November he boarded a stage at Johnny Owens' ranch and rode it down to the Chug. At the Chug he found an unattended freighter's camp and appropriated for himself three mules and a gun, then decamped for parts unknown.[18]

Another party that made "Persimmon Bill's" acquaintance on the road was given a slightly different, and probably a more reliable, account of Sergeant Sullivan's death. A band of Arapaho Indians camped near Fort Fetterman reported the theft of some horses, and the theft was traced to "Persimmon Bill" and William Madden, a deserter. Sergeant Sullivan was dispatched to retrieve the horses and arrest the thieves. Sullivan insisted on "Persimmon Bill's" arrest, and

Medicine Bow, stagecoach and six passengers. *(Photo: Courtesy of Union Pacific Railroad Museum.)*

although Bill warned Sullivan to go back, he read the order for their arrest. The sergeant then raised his gun, which was already cocked, but "Persimmon Bill" was the first to fire. Madden was later arrested at Medicine Bow by Lieutenant Crittenden, but "Persimmon Bill" remained at large.

To this party "Persimmon Bill" also claimed that he was "the leading spirit of a regularly organized band of horse thieves" that extended from the Black Hills to the San Juan's in Colorado.

At this point in the narrative "Persimmon Bill" is reported to be "in the Hills, and when not engaged in his thieving business, loafs about the towns there, having plenty of money and spending it freely."

Back at Abney's stable, our narrator is about to answer the question, "How did he look?".

Oh, there was little or nothing about him either in dress or physiognomy to indicate the frontier bully or desperado. He was about 31 or 32 years of age. About five feet-eight or ten inches high; rather well built; would weigh perhaps 140 pounds; had short, thick arms and a short, bull shaped neck. His hair was dark brown, and was cut short; eyes bright blue; small, well-shaped nose; thin lips, shaded by a small blonde mustache. His chin was covered by a short brown beard, which covered the lower portion of his face. The only features indicating his ferocious disposition was his very heavy, projecting eyebrows and his thick, heavy lower jaws.

How did he treat us, did you say? Oh, pretty well; he treated me better than the balance of the boys. I shall never forget his exhibition of marksmanship the morning we were turned loose to come on to Cheyenne. He took us out of camp aways, and picking out a cottonwood tree as a mark, which stood about forty yards away, he took two navy revolvers in his hands, and holding them at arms' length, fired every cartridge at the tree *without cocking the pistols*. He merely pulled the hammers of the pistols back and let them go, never stopping to pull a trigger. The twelve shots sent out of his two holster pistols seemed like one continuous discharge from a mitrailleuse. He fired from his other two revolvers shot after shot, each after whirling round on his heel and without apparently taking aim; but he seldom, if ever, missed his mark. He was equally skillful with his two rifles, one of which he carried swung upon the left side of his saddle, the other hanging by his right hip.

Before bidding Bill farewell, I told him to look out for his neck, as the boys in the Hills and the soldiers were looking for him. The good natured young renegade laughed ironically as he replied, "Tell the folks in the States I will see them at the Centennial."[20] And then, in a more serious tone, he said as he rode by the wagon side, "I don't know whether I can get out of this country or not. I want to quit this life as soon as I can make a raise to go east on." He acknowledged that he expected to "be hung" when caught, but reiterated in his long conversation his determination to die before being taken. He said, just before shaking hands with his *unwilling guests:* "Tell Gen. Bradley you have spent a night with Persimmon Bill, and tell him how I treated you. You can tell the old boy I am gone to Custer City to finish that half-breed, Jules Simons, who boasts he'll take my hair and get that reward. Good-bye, boys; don't forget Bill Chambers."

And then he turned his beautiful bay horse towards the Black Hills and soon disappeared on the trail of his red allies.

A telegram to the Cheyenne Daily Leader from Fort Laramie, dateline April 5, stated: "Persimmon Bill, the outlaw, made his appearance in a camp five miles south of Hat Creek, five days ago. He had supper and breakfast, and stayed overnight in the camp. When last heard of he was at Raw Hide Buttes, very drunk, and having considerable money."[21]

Robbery was a daily occurrence on the road between Cheyenne and Custer the spring of '76. No doubt Persimmon Bill had taken in a small party and spent the proceeds of the robbery on a monumental binge. Small parties traveling the route to the new El Dorado were easy prey for the road agents, and many of the robberies were not reported. Exceptions were when well-known persons were robbed, a large amount of money was taken, or murder. One party, going against the tide, counted 1,063 persons "on the road" between the two places.[22]

On April 16, 1876 the Metz family and their servant, Mrs. Rachel Briggs, were robbed, murdered, and horribly mutilated in Red Canyon near Custer. The crime was generally attributed to Indians, but some thought hostiles should have been spelled "hoss-steals." Jesse Brown, one of the men who helped move the bodies, stated that he found boot and shoe marks where the attackers had lain in ambush. That some, at least, of the band were Indians there is little doubt. William "California Bill" Felton, traveling with — but ahead of — the Metz', stated that those who had attacked him were Indians.[23]

Three days after the "Metz Massacre," veteran stage man H. E. "Stuttering" Brown was shot from ambush north of Hat Creek. Brown, one of four men traveling in a fast freight wagon, was the only man shot at, as if he were singled-out. The bullet first struck a brass cartridge in his belt and both entered his left hip. General Luther Bradley dispatched Acting Assistant Surgeon Pettys from Ft. Laramie with an ambulance and escort, but the wound proved fatal. Pettys' report stated that Brown died on the 25th, the ball traveling upward and cutting the intestine. Before he died, Brown said that it was imperative that he speak with Luke Voorhees. Although Voorhees made a gallant effort to arrive at Ft. Laramie, he was too late. Brown had had words with a road agent that had been operating along the route a few days before his death. Brown had threatened to kill the road agent, and in turn, "Persimmon Bill" told Brown he would "get" him.

Was Persimmon Bill all bad? Ed Lemmon states that "Persimmon Bill" was pronounced the "prince of them all," inasmuch as he did not rob women. That is, if he was sure that the valuables belonged

to her. If he thought she had been given them to carry through the outlaw infested country "Persimmon Bill" made 'em his. Lemmon states that "Persimmon Bill" was so adept at disguising himself that it was hard to identify him, although "nearly everyone knew who he was."

Lawyer Charles Potter was among the party "taken in" by Persimmon Bill. Potter later defended Dunc Blackburn's former partner, Clark Pelton, when he was tried for the murder of Adolph Cuny. (*Photo: Courtesy Wyoming State Archives, Museums, and Historical Department.*)

"Judge" William Kuykendell, who knew "Persimmon Bill" in Cheyenne, credited him with saving him from being robbed while on the road between Cheyenne and Custer City. In fact, "Persimmon Bill" had heard where he planned to camp, and skipped the place Kuykendell had picked out when he raided several camps later that night.[25]

Not long after the murder of "Stuttering" Brown, "Persimmon Bill" quit the road. Reasons given for his abrupt departure vary, but he may have made a big enough "raise" to quit as he wished to do. Nick Janise said that he died in Red Canyon, at the hands of one of his own band. It would be fitting, but a more likely account was given to Ed Lemmon by A. M. "Cap" Willard shortly before the latter's death. Willard told Lemmon that after he quit, he returned to North Carolina, married, and began a life of respectability.

1. As will be seen, our unidentified narrator had an intimate knowledge of "Persimmon Bill." Obviously a reporter, or at least a newspaper correspondent, at the time, he gained favor with "Persimmon Bill" by his occupation. While it is impossible to confirm several of the incidents, it is more important that nothing in the narrative can be disproven.

2. It is possible that these Indians had met with Crook prior to the entry of the Crook Expedition into the Big Horn Mountains. At any rate, the March date does not coincide with John F. Finerty, **War-Path and Bivouac**, which states on page 79, that they first camped at the foothills on June 5. John C. Bourke, **On the Border With Crook**, p. 291, states the Big Horns were first seen by them on June 1, and p. 307, states they broke camp and headed westward on June 16.

3. The name Murphysville has been shortened to Murphy. W. C. Allen, **The Annals of Haywood County, North Carolina,** states that James Chambers, the father of three sons, Joseph, William, and Elihu, was the first of the family to settle in North Carolina. Although William, the son of James, could not have been our "Persimmon Bill," of him it is said: William was a man of adventure, went to the northeast, engaged in the Indian Wars of that early period . . . (and) finally settled down in the middle west and made his home there."

4. The incomplete **North Carolina Troops 1861-1865** does not record any Chambers in the 23rd regiment.

5. This deserting one outfit, or even one army, then joining another was not unusual.

6. This is not readily verifiable. Doubtless scenes like this were enacted not only at Bowling Green, but throughout the countryside.

7. From July 2 through July 26, 1863, General John H. Morgan commanded his men on raids into Kentucky, Indiana, and Ohio. On July 19 the largest part of Morgan's forces were captured, killed, or wounded at Blennerhasset Island in the Ohio River. The remainder surrendered July 26, near New Lisbon. Confederate losses: 2,000 men killed, wounded, or captured. Survivors were imprisoned at Johnson's Island.

8. Robert G. Athearn, **Union Pacific Country,** p. 65, states rails were laid into Cheyenne November 13, 1867.

9. For a partial account of the vigilante movement in Cheyenne, see Lola M. Homsher, (ed.), **South Pass, 1868,** pp. 15-24.

10. Russell H. White, **Historical Review of the Woodbury County Sheriff's Department,** pp. 4-6, lends some credence to this incident. While not specifically mentioned, John McDonald was elected to the first of his four terms in 1871. His brother Dan served as his deputy throughout his tenure as sheriff.

11. L. G. "Pat" Flannery, ed., **John Hunton's Diary,** Vol. 2, p. 102, entry for June 6, 1876, states, in part: "Telegram from U.S. Deputy Marshall (sic) about Jules Seminole." Jules Seminole is variously spelled in a number of books.

12. The words "shot down" and "killed" are not, of course, synonymous.

13. Sherman was a short-lived "Hell on Wheels" town between Laramie and Cheyenne.

14. Bourke, op. cit., p. 254, states: "On the 1st of March . . . we left Fort Fetterman."

15. Finerty, op. cit., p. 52, identifies Major Chambers as Major Alexander Chambers.

16. The **Cheyenne Daily Leader,** March 5, 1876 states that Sullivan was shot in the back by at least one of two shots. It further states that his body was robbed of "considerable money" and a gun.

17. **Cheyenne Daily Leader,** March 9, 1875.

18. **Cheyenne Daily Leader,** December 4, 1875.

19. **Cheyenne Daily Leader,** March 16, April 21, 1876.

20. The Centennial Exhibition opened in Philadelphia, May 10. Perhaps "Persimmon Bill" was reiterating his desire to return to "the States" with a May 10 date in mind.

21. **Cheyenne Daily Leader,** April 6, 1876.

22. **Cheyenne Daily Leader,** March 5, 1876.

23. George Lathrop, **Some Pioneer Recollections,** p. 34, contains a graphic description of the mutilation. John S. McClintock, **Pioneer Days in the Black Hills,** p. 59, and Brown and Willard, **The Black Hills Trails,** p. 57, both add information about the possible participation of white men in the crime.

24. "Medical Record, Ft. Laramie 1868-1879", Ft. Laramie National Historic Site. Agnes Wright Spring, **Cheyenne-Black Hills Stage and Express Routes,** p. 138. **Cheyenne Daily Leader,** April 25 (two articles).

25. W. L. Kuykendall, **Frontier Days,** pp. 175-176.

26. **Boss Cowman,** The Recollections of Ed Lemmon, 1857-1946. Nellie Snyder Yost, ed., p. 83.

LAME JOHNNY

"There came to the Hills in the Spring of 1876, a young man who wore the handle of Lame Johnny, and as a promoter of diversified industries, I think he wore the blue ribbon." So began "Doc" Peirce's narrative about Lame Johnny. Peirce related that Lame Johnny, whose name in the states he learned later was Cornelius Donahue, was known in the Hills as John Hurley, but had several names that "did not belong to him." Lame Johnny was "a civil and topographical engineer; a No. 1 bookkeeper; pretty fair in music; (and) was a splendid judge of a horse," to which he added, "no matter who owned it."[1]

Lame Johnny grew to trust Peirce and told him that he was from Philadelphia and had received his education at Girard College, but refused to tell Peirce his true name: "It wouldn't do you any good to know . . ."[2] Girard College was founded in 1833 with a $6 million bequest in the will of a Philadelphia entrepreneur Stephen Girard as a home for fatherless boys up to the age of eighteen.[3] Records indicate that Cornelius Donahue, born October 6, 1854, entered Girard College on January 21, 1862.[4]

In 1871, his last full academic year at Girard, Cornelius Donahue was named to the school's highest class of honor, the "Third Class of Honor." To be eligible for the distinction the student's conduct, rated from zero to ten, could be no lower than 9.7 for the year. In 1871 Cornelius Donahue's conduct was rated 9.81, and he scored 9.27 academically.[5] Many of the abilities Peirce found in Lame Johnny can be attributed to the curriculum at Girard. The 1872 "Annual Report" reveals that classes were given in: French; Spanish; Natural History; General Physics; Mathematics, which included surveying; and

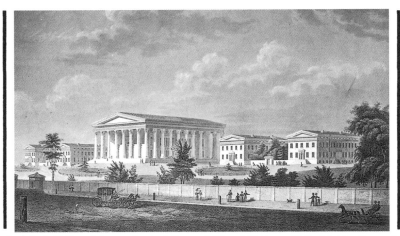

Founder's Hall and four outer buildings of Girard College, Philadelphia, Pennsylvania. Girard, trader, merchant and banker left funds in his will to support the college for "poor, white orphans" between the ages of six and eighteen. Since opening its doors over 18,000 boys have been admitted. *(Photo: Courtesy Girard College.)*

Graphics, which included bookkeeping. Music, not listed but no doubt given, was perhaps not thought of as a class, per se.[6] Records also show that Cornelius Donahue left Girard on October 6, 1872, that being the day he reached eighteen years of age.[7]

Peirce found there was "something mysterious in that young man's make up" that excited his curiosity. Peirce became a confidant of the "hard to get acquainted with" young man who possessed a "retiring disposition" and Lame Johnny told him:

> . . . after leaving school (I) drifted to Texas, where I engaged myself to a rich, old cattleman who agreed to give me a share in the increase of stock for my services. I worked hard and was doing nicely and had earned about seven hundred head of my own brand[8] when one moonlight night the Comanche Indians made a raid up our way and drove off all my stock. That discouraged me. I went over to see old Caststeel, (C)hief of the Tongaway (sic) Indians and made medicine with him, in regard to going down and visiting the Comanches. He listened until I was through talking, studied for a few minutes and then arose and said: "My people are few in numbers but they are brave. We will go with you; but our tribe raids on dark night(s). Wait until the moon changes and then come."[9]
> The first dark night I struck out, the Indians going along. We

made a pretty good haul — sixty head of horses which I disposed of, and divided the proceeds with the Indians. That trip gave me a taste of adventure and I have been working ever since to get even for the loss of my cattle . . .[10]

By the account Lame Johnny gave Peirce, he then "drifted north with the Kansas crowd and settled on Castle Creek and tried mining" when he arrived in the Black Hills. After the Indians raided the miner's horses Lame Johnny spent the summer trading horses with them. He hadn't planned it that way, but, "I would run them in and they would run them back to the Agency." He served as a deputy sheriff of Custer County, and "proved to be a very efficient officer of the law" according to Jesse Brown.[11]

His "office in the woods" from which he dealt in horses was lucrative, but he grew tired of "the stock business" and was hired as a bookkeeper for Homestake. His employment lasted until an acquaintance, for whatever reason, "addressed him as a horse thief from Texas." Lame Johnny said that, "a man whom I offended, by refusing to let him sell my Indian ponies, he to keep all over six dollars apiece. I was getting as high as one hundred twenty dollars a pair, so I refused his generous offer. He remarked at the time he would get even with me." Lame Johnny concluded, "I guess he did."[12]

Whether Lame Johnny actually left Texas under a cloud or not, the **Chicago Times'** correspondent at Fort Robinson, Nebraska, said in a "special":

. . . After committing several murders in Texas, in the last of which he was severely wounded, being shot through both limbs, making him a cripple for life, from which he derived the sourbriquet (sic) of "Lame Johnny," he left that state three years ago and came to this country to start anew . . .[13]

The **Black Hills Journal** also reported that "he was drove out of Texas some years ago by a vigilance committee . . ." and followed the story of the gunshot wound. Although not verbatim, it appears that the **Black Hills Journal's** source of information was an earlier **Chicago Times** article that mentioned Lame Johnny's "thieving exploits."[14]

Lame Johnny told Peirce that he had fallen from a horse which had caused the injury, a statement agreed to by Brown and Willard's **The Black Hills Trails.**[15] It was testified to in a court hearing that Lame Johnny had been required to leave a deposit with a Cheyenne cobbler for a pair of shoes that he ordered. The deposit was required for once made, the shoes would have been unsalable to anyone else:

they were sized 6 and 4. A gunshot wound, three years old at most, could hardly have caused such a disparity in sizes.[16] Lame Johnny admitted that his experience in Texas had given him "a taste of adventure," but said nothing about a vigilance committee to Peirce.

Lame Johnny quit the Homestake, and nothing was heard of him for quite some time. He had returned to the "stock business" and had added miners and ranchers horses to his "line of merchandise." One of his raids resulted in "Little Brocky's Last Raid," while yet another resulted in a warrant for stock stealing being issued for his arrest in Laramie County, Wyoming. Lame Johnny added stagecoach robbery to his "diversified industries," which led **Corn Country** author Homer Croy to state, "thus showing to what depths a college education will lead."[17]

Dr. Valentine T. McGillycuddy had signed a warrant for Lame Johnny's arrest for the theft of Indian ponies. *(Photo: Courtesy South Dakota State Historical Society.)*

The first stage robbery that Lame Johnny was identified in occurred between French Creek and Buffalo Gap, at a site later known as Lame Johnny Creek. The **Black Hills Daily Times** reported:

> On the arrival of Sidney stage this afternoon, we learned that the coach, which left here on Thursday last, was attacked by road agents between French Creek and Buffalo Gap, and that Mr. Ed Cooke, the Division Agent, was slightly wounded in the ear, from a shot fired by one of the robbers. As near as we can learn, Mr. Cooke was inside the coach at the time, and was holding a child, in consequence of which he was unable to alight quick enough to satisfy the highwaymen, one of whom

fired into the coach with the result already mentioned. So far as spoils are concerned, we cannot ascertain the exact amount taken by the agents, but are informed that it was small. Mr. Jorgin, late agent for Clark's Sidney express, and his partner drove up in a buggy just as the coach was stopped, and the robbers called on these gentlemen to throw up their hands, which they very promptly acceded to, and were at once relieved of their gold sacks and pistols.[18]

Ed Cooke had recognized Lame Johnny, and told his messengers to be on the lookout for him.[19] Lame Bradley, the man who shot Cooke, escaped the noose of a Black Hills vigilante committee and the guns of Boone May, but fell in Texas. He was killed by a youth of about nineteen, whom he tried to rob.[20]

Lame Johnny and Frank Harris were arrested at or near Ft. Robinson by "Whispering" Smith, a sometimes Union Pacific detective, stock detective, and Laramie County lawman, for "leading away some halters with horses in them." About a week before his arrest he had stolen some horses from W. M. Ward in the Custer vicinity, and had taken them to Fort Robinson, where they were "gobbled for stealing a government bridle." Ward telegraphed military officials at Ft. Robinson to hold them, and upon the arrival of Smith, Lame Johnny was turned over to him. It was decided to take Lame Johnny to Rapid City for trial. John B. Furay, Special Agent for the Post Office Department, described the scene before they departed:[21]

> . . . Johnny, it seems, had a good keen scent of danger and so in quitting Camp Robinson, he took time by the forelock and bade his companions a long and, as he predicted, a 'last' farewell. He evidently felt a sort of premonition, as it were, that something would interfere with his longevity . . .[22]

At the Red Cloud stage station Jesse Brown assumed charge of Lame Johnny, and Smith rode on the front boot with the driver. Near Buffalo Gap Brown noticed that Lame Johnny had become "restless and nervous." Upon inquiry, Lame Johnny revealed his fear that the horseman they had seen riding parallel with the stage was Boone May. Brown concurred with Lame Johnny's identification. Brown left the stage at Buffalo Gap and Smith regained custody of Lame Johnny. Brown had to return his horse to Battle Creek, and was behind the stage when it entered Dry Creek.[23] From Smith's account:

> . . . The mob consisted of about eight men — anyway, no more came in view; though, as the locality is marked by a

dense growth of bushes, others may have been concealed. There were in the coach, at the time, Mr. Smith, his prisoner, and a lady and two children. Mr. Smith said he knew from the beginning that they were not robbers, from their general bearing and their manner of stopping the coach — they were scattered, and evidently wished to avoid hurting anyone in the coach or being hurt themselves. "Where are them thieves?" was the first demand. "I have a prisoner in here," answered Mr. Smith. "Bring him out," was the next demand, "he is the one we are after." Mr. Smith . . . got out of the stage to remonstrate; but was compelled to stand aside by the crowd . . . They then took the prisoner out of the coach and carried him a hundred yards away. Mr. Smith then, being now unarmed, the crowd having compelled him to throw his arms on the ground — started to go where the prisoner was being held; but was stopped on the way and ordered to return to the coach. He then requested them to allow him to take his handcuffs from the prisoner; and this, after some objection from a few, he was finally allowed to do; and then he was again ordered to at once return to the coach . . .[24]

In addition, the **Black Hills Daily Times** reported that:
. . . the doomed robber resisted the vigilantes with all his strength and begged the officer, who had him in charge, for his revolver. He knew well his fate and wanted to sell his life as dearly as possible.[25]

Smith, who could hardly be faulted for not giving his revolvers to Lame Johnny, spent the next fifteen to twenty minutes searching for his revolvers, apparently oblivious to everything else.[26]

Once in the hands of the vigilantes Lame Johnny's chances were "about equal to a thousand to one":
(they) demanded from him a confession and the names of his associates in crime. He replied that he had nothing to confess and never would betray a partner, whereupon they told him his hour had come, as they intended to hang him. He replied: "Hang and be damned; you can't do it any too soon."[27]

The "lady and two children" were identified by Jesse Brown as his wife and daughters. Brown was following the stage at the time, and was joined by his wife and daughters who ran back to him. They were soon joined by Smith who asked for and received, Brown's horse.[28] It is interesting to note that the only time Smith had custody of Lame

Johnny after leaving the Red Cloud station was after Boone May had been recognized, and Brown again boarded the stage after the prisoner was lynched.

"The last resting place of Lame Johnnie the Noted Black Hills Highwayman, Buffalo Gap, S.D." One of the minor controversies surrounding the lynching of Lame Johnny has been the kind of tree that he was suspended from. This photo should provide the answer. *(Photo: Courtesy Nebraska State Historical Society.)*

The body of Lame Johnny was buried the next day by a passing freight outfit. It was the same day that Harris was to start to Rapid City. Furay's report stated:

> ... Harris ... having heard of Lame Johnny's misfortune it is alleged that he, too, felt something of a premonition and more especially about the time they were approaching the tree and the grave of Lame Johnny. Harris afterwards stated to me that he felt he was gone . . .[29]

Within a few days of the lynching, thought to have been committed by "victims of 'Lame Johnny's' rascalities" from Battle Creek and Custer, someone nailed an epitaph written on a board, to the tree:

> Pilgrim, Pause. You're standing on
> The moldering clay of 'Limping John.'
> Tread lightly, stranger, on his sod
> For if he moves, you're robbed by G-d.[30]

Harris safely reached Rapid City despite his premonition, where he was landed in jail. Among the prisoners in jail at the time were Fritz Staurck and John McDonald, indicted for the June 9 robbery of the coach at Dry Creek, six miles north of Buffalo Gap.[31] Arrested in Deadwood, they were indicted for the robbery in mid-August at Rapid City. Furay reported to his superiors that, "I never worked harder in my life than I did in working up and getting present the witnesses who professed to have a knowledge of the circumstances by which their guilt was made manifest."[32]

John B. Furay, Special Agent for the Post Office Department was investigating the theft of registered mail during the June 9, 1879 stagecoach robbery. Furay also advised William H. H. Llewellyn to take Boone May along "for safety" when he went after Curly Grimes. *(Photo: Courtesy Western History Research Center, University of Wyoming.)*

Col. W. H. Parker, defense attorney for McDonald and Staurck. *(Photo: Courtesy South Dakota State Historical Society.)*

McDonald and Staurck were tried in territorial court for highway robbery then the court, with the same judge, organized as a U.S. Court in which they were tried for robbing the mails. Furay stated: "I do not think there was a man in the courtroom who sincerely believed their guilt as proven, but the jury said 'guilty' and that settled it." McDonald and Staurck were to be sentenced, and with that case over, the case of Frank Harris came before the bench.[33]

Harris was found guilty of stealing Indian ponies in U.S. Court, and of grand larceny under the Territorial laws. Prior to sentencing the presiding judge asked Harris if he had anything to say. "Yes, before your honor sentences me, I shall have something to say." Harris arose and confessed that he, with Lame Johnny and Tom Moore were the men who had committed the robbery McDonald and Staurck had just been found guilty of. In an affidavit Harris stated:

> We, Lame Johnny and Tom Moore robbed the coach on the 9th of January, 1879, at Dry (C)reek, six miles this side of Buffalo Gap. We laid at the point where we robbed the coach from about 4 o'clock that evening. I stood on the off side of the coach; I stopped the coach; Tom Moore went through the passengers; Lame Johnnie stood on the opposite me and made the passengers throw up their hands; while they were going through the passengers after I stopped the driver I sat down behind a bush out of sight; Tom Moore, whilst going through the passengers was addressed several times of No. 2; we got two silver watches, one open face stem winder silver watch with a kind of flashy brass chain; the man that gave up that watch asked for his pocketbook to get back his marriage badge which was given to him; Lame Johnny gave that watch to Goodwin, the blacksmith at Custer, for grub; I think the other silver watch I kept and afterwards gave to Johnny at Cheyenne, to get a pair of boots with: after the passengers got out, Moore went through the coach and found the gold watch with a name inside of it — Capt. Adair, the initials I forget; Moore kept that watch; Johnnie took the stamps, which was most all that we got; there was some small change, not more than $10 or $15; there were three $2 bills I know; the name of Hooper was on the stem winding silver watch; I heard Sam tell the man with the long duster on, who was Hooper, to take off the watch chain, for he could not take it off without tearing his coat. Then there was a Dutchman in the outfit; he made a remark about being tired holding up his hands; Moore said if he did not dry up he would leave him there; a little fellow that rode on the outside with the driver Moore asked the tall man what he was doing with that boy for a partner; the little fellow, Abbott, said that he was no boy; then Moore went through him; there was a whiskey flask and a small revolver found in the coach; both silver watches were open face, and now since I think of it, it was the Dutchman asked for the badge.

After the passengers were gone through, the driver asked for the spring that held the candle; he said he wanted to put it back in its place; Moore said never mind, he would take care of it. Then Moore ordered him to pitch off the mail sacks, which he did; the passengers were then ordered back into the coach, and the driver ordered to drive on. The coach left and we cut the mail sacks open and found a bunch of stamps and several registered letters, but no money in any of them. We left the sacks in the road, and left a pair of box-toed shoes that we found in the sacks. We then went down toward Buffalo Gap, to the crossing of Beaver (C)reek. Moore left us there, and Johnnie and I went to Custer. Moore said he was going to Sidney. We rode from where we left Moore about two miles on to Custer road and camped until morning on Beaver (C)reek. Johnnie burned the stamps there in the morning. We laid outside of Custer City for two or three days, and went into town at night to get grub. We made arrangements with French Billy to get us horses and meet us at a spring about two miles from Custer City. He brought two horses, a black and a dun, to us about midnight. I rode the dun and Johnnie rode the black. We gave Billy the little revolver and left our horses, a brown and a sorrel, there, which Billy said he would look after and take care of until we came back.[34]

Harris told the court where his remaining share of the loot was, and it was found just where he said it was. "And then," Furay reported, "there was the devil to pay sure enough!"[35]

A soldier testified that he had redeemed a watch that Lame Johnny had left "in soak" to the cobbler, and produced it in court. The watch was identified by Frank Abbott as the one stolen from him the night of June 9.[36]

Staurck and McDonald's attorney motioned for a new trial which was granted. After the prosecution nolled the case, they were released. Once out of jail, they found that they had not only been the victims of the courts, but also the criminals: two weeks after their release, they were still searching for their "outfits."[37]

Furay reported that about half the people believed that Staurck and McDonald were innocent, while the other half thought that the penitentiary bound Harris had saved them, and may have even been their partners.[38]

Harris, a man about 23 years old, whose "demeanor throughout was that of a reckless, hardened criminal apparently thought that the judge would look kindly upon his confession, which the judge acknowledged might have prevented innocent men from serving time for crimes they didn't commit. Harris "venfully kicked out one of his legs as far as the shackling chains" would allow, and hissed, "Jesus Christ," when he was sentenced to an aggregate of five years.[39]

Ed Lemmon, in **Boss Cowman** related that a cowboy who worked for him robbed the grave of Lame Johnny of the skull, some gold teeth, and the high-heeled boot. The cowboy was fired for his actions, and ordered to return his gruesome relics, but Lemmon was of the opinion they went back east with the cowboy.[40]

About four years after that incident, lightning struck the limb from which Lame Johnny had been hung, and it dropped to his grave. Interpreted by some as a signal from God that an innocent man had been hung, Lemmon felt that "if Johnny hadn't committed the crime he was hung for he was guilty of enough others to warrant the hanging." It seemed to be the opinion of the majority.[41]

1. Ellis Taylor Peirce, "Odd Characters and Incidents in the Black Hills during the '70's", manuscript in the South Dakota Historical Society, Pierre, South Dakota.

2. Ibid.

3. **Encyclopedia Britanica,** Vol. IV, p. 553; **Encyclopedia Americana,** Vol. 12, p. 760. At the time of his death in 1831, his $7 million fortune was the largest in the nation. Founded in 1833, Girard College opened its doors in 1848.

4. John A. Lander, President, Girard College, Philadelphia, Pennsylvania to author, October 30, 1979.

    According to Ward J. Childs, Archivist III, Department of Records, City of Philadelphia, the city did not begin keeping birth records until 1860. Childs to author, February 7, 1980.

    A "Cornelius Donahue" appears in the 1850 Pennsylvania Census, and "Donahue, Mary, wid. Cornelius" appears in an 1864 city directory. This seems to indicate that Cornelius and Mary Donahue were his parents, although this has not been definitely established.

5. **Second Annual Report of the Directors of City Trusts,** pp. 55 and 72.

6. **Third Annual Report of the Directors of City Trusts,** pp. 59-61.

7. Lander to author, op. cit. Although Lame Johnny is frequently referred to as a "college graduate," Mr. Lander stated, "He did not graduate from Girard College, but left in 1872 because he was over age." In the account Lame Johnny told Peirce, he used the words "educated at" in reference to Girard College.

8. This seems to be an exageration. Even if cattle were valued at $20 a head, Lame Johnny would have earned in excess of $200 a month.

9. There is a certain amount of truth in the words attributed to Chief Caststeel. In 1862 the Tonkawa Indians numbered about 300.

Through "warfare and hardship" their numbers had dwindled to ninety-seven before they were taken to Ft. Griffin, Texas, in 1884. Walter Prescott Webb, (ed.), **The Handbook of Texas,** Vol. II, pp. 788-9.

10. Peirce, op. cit.
11. Peirce, op. cit.; Brown and Willard; **The Black Hills Trails,** p. 298.
12. Peirce, op. cit.; Brown and Willard, op. cit., p. 299.
13. The **Sidney** (Nebraska) **Telegraph,** July 12, 1879 reprinted the **Chicago Times** article. The reprinted article makes reference to an earlier article that was not reprinted in the **Sidney Telegraph.**
14. **Black Hills Journal,** July 5, 1879.
15. Lame Johnny, in the account given Peirce, makes no mention of a brother as does Brown and Willard, op. cit., p. 298.
16. **Black Hills Daily Times,** February 10, 1880.
17. Homer Croy, **Corn Country,** p. 110; Brown and Willard, op. cit., p. 299; Peirce, op. cit.
18. **Black Hills Daily Times,** August 25, 1877.
19. Brown and Willard, p. 299.
20. **Black Hills Journal,** November 23, 1878.
21. Dr. Valentine T. McGillycuddy, "Black Hills Names", **South Dakota Historical Collections,** Vol. 6 (1912), p. 274; The reports of John B. Furay, Special Agent for the Post Office Department, in the National Archives, were printed in full in Agnes Wright Spring, "Who Robbed the Mail Coach?", **Frontier Times,** August-September 1967, pp. 25, 58-59. Because these reports (two) are more accessible in this form, hereinafter they will be cited as Spring. **Black Hills Daily Times,** July 8, 1879.
22. Spring, op. cit.
23. Brown and Willard, op. cit., pp. 300-301.
24. **Black Hills Journal,** July 5, 1879.
25. **Black Hills Daily Times,** July 8, 1879.
26. **Black Hills Journal,** July 5, 1879.
27. **Sidney Telegraph,** July 12, 1879.
28. Brown and Willard, op. cit., pp. 300-301.
29. Spring, op. cit.
30. Jesse Brown, in **The Black Hills Trails,** p. 301, attributes authorship of the epitaph to Furay, while Furay, in his report, stated that "someone" had nailed it up. The exact wording differs, and preference was given to Furay's wording as his report was written shortly thereafter.
31. **Black Hills Journal,** June 15, 1878. Spring, op. cit.
32. Spring, op. cit.
33. Spring, op. cit.; **Black Hills Journal,** September 16, 1879.
34. **Black Hills Daily Times,** February 10, 1880.
35. **Black Hills Journal,** September 16, 1879; Spring, op. cit.
36. **Black Hills Daily Times,** February 10, 1880.
37. Ibid.; **Black Hills Journal,** September 16, 1879; Spring, op. cit.
38. Spring, op. cit.
39. **Black Hills Journal,** August 30, 1879.
40. Nellie Snyder Yost (ed.), **Boss Cowman;** The Recollections of Ed Lemmon 1857-1946, pp. 106-7.
41. Ibid.; The **Black Hills Daily Times,** July 8, 1879, seemed to echo the prevelant feeling when it stated, "Lame Johnny, a road agent, horse thief and a bad man on general principles . . ."

"LENGTHY" JOHNSON

Had horse thieves, as nobility, been titled, "Lengthy" Johnson would have been proclaimed "King Lengthy of the Northern Black Hills." As it was, he was a "good sleek one" who was "the terror of Spearfish Valley." William Wallace Johnson, who sailed under the aliases of "Long," "Lengthy," "Gus," and "James E.," had only one redeeming feature in the eyes of one law and order Deadwood newspaper editor — an abundance of "broad, open frankness."[1]

Johnson's peculiar brand of frankness first began to surface about midnight, September 9, 1878, between Lightning Creek and the Cheyenne River when three armed men stopped the "down" (Cheyenne bound) coach. The coach contained four passengers and messenger Gene Smith. Smith remained in the coach and intended to "stand them off," but one of the trio placed a passenger between himself and Smith and advanced to the coach. Under the threat of death to the passenger, Smith was compelled to surrender. With the robbery of the passengers completed, the unabashed three were in the process of plundering the mail sacks when the "up" (Deadwood bound)) coach arrived on the scene. It, too, was overhauled by the road agents. Nearly one hundred dollars, some jewelry and watches were "on the dump," but like Oliver Twist, they hollered for more. The stage company, ever fearful that revealing how much was obtained from the treasure box would only encourage more robberies, declined to comment on their losses.[2]

Masks had been looked upon as formalities by the road agents, and it had been a very informal hold-up. One was easily recognized as "James E." Johnson, and he was apprehended by military authorities

at Camp Robinson, Nebraska. Deputy U.S. Marshal F. O. Horn met
military officials at Sidney, Nebraska, and the transfer of custody was
completed. After the arrival of Horn and his prisoner in Cheyenne,
"James E." was remembered as "Lengthy" — someone who had
loafed about Cheyenne the previous spring, and "not a stranger to our
police force."[3]

When Johnson was taken into custody he said the $100 bill in his
possession was given him by Ed Cook, the superintendent of the stage
line's northern division. However, he was suspected of starting a campaign against the truth when he claimed it was remuneration for
"work" he had performed. Johnson later revised his story and said it
was part of the proceeds from the sale of his ranch. However, he
steadfastly maintained he was "James E." Johnson, an honest former
ranchman from near the Red Cloud Agency.[4]

"James E." then did a complete turnabout, and admitted that he
was "the original 'Lengthy' Johnson" and claimed all others were
"spurious — mere imitators." He said he was from Rochester, New
York, and had lived in the Rocky Mountains Region for the past thirteen years. The **Cheyenne Daily Leader** reported that Johnson was
well educated, quite witty, and "looked very much like other men"
except that he was exceedingly tall, looming up about six feet four
inches. Johnson said that he was sure "there is a mistake
somewhere," and felt confident that he would be honorably
acquitted.[5]

"Lengthy" was soon habeaus corpused out of limbo on $5,000
bond and spent the majority of his time wandering around Cheyenne,
showering benedictions upon everyone connected with his arrest, including the local scribes who had chronicled his recent troubles for
posterity.[6]

One reporter who "Lengthy" felt had been particularly insensitive to his difficulties received a personal visit. "Lengthy" admitted to
the reporter that while he was on his ranch he had formed the acquain-
tances of men who were "on the rush," but Johnson maintained that
such were made during legitimate business deals. He sold them grain
and provisions, that was his business; he was there to make money and
these men always paid him his price — cash money. He pointed out
that other ranchmen in the vicinity could do likewise if they wished,
but he reckoned that they wouldn't. Johnson asserted that he could
make a living from his ranch, and didn't need to supplement his in-
come by robbing stagecoaches. He added that, had he not been

"treated so d----d mean," he would have put the authorities on the track of some men he knew who did rob the stages.[7]

Johnson's call on the reporter met with partial success. The insensitive one admitted, "When he says this, it is hard, from his appearance, to doubt the truth of his assertions," but added that if Johnson wasn't a road agent, perhaps he should be charged as an accomplice for his uncommunicativeness.[8]

While Johnson was temporarily indisposed in Cheyenne he read that he was still a "resident" of Spearfish Valley, and visited "the metropolis of that section" whenever he wished. Johnson was "a good sleek one" right enough, but not even he was that "sleek." He was, however, "sleek" enough to be released by the Cheyenne authorities for lack of evidence; even after he confessed that he was "the original." With Johnson it was simply a case of "out of the fat and into the fire."[9]

Rustling had reached such epidemic proportions in Spearfish Valley that a vigilance committee was formed in July of 1878. After its formation, Frank Cashner, Spearfish merchant and the group's self-appointed spokesman, said it was the committee's sole intention to "break up the gang or strangle every suspicious son of a gun in that country." With a sly wink Cashner added that one rustler had already "been fixed so he couldn't run off any more stock."[10] The **Black Hills Daily Times** offered the opinion that the vigilantes could have little effect on the rustlers while they were permitted to "slip around and among (the vigilantes) with the greatest indifference."[11]

The **Times** was correct in its assumption. The vigilantes had no marked effect on the rustlers until the night of September 18th, when "Lengthy" Johnson, the biggest fish of them all, threw them a couple of little fish — George W. Keating and Orbean Davis.

Davis owned a ranch on Spearfish Mountain and worked as a corral keeper at Gayville. Outside of Spearfish he was known as a real "rustler" as those who possessed an unusual amount of ambition were referred to. To the citizens of Spearfish, Davis' ranch was known as a rendezvous for the many stock artists who operated in the Valley.[12]

George W. Keating, the proprietor of a butcher shop at Central City, near Deadwood, did not possess such an enviable reputation. He had been arrested several times for the possession of stolen stock, and although it was never proven, it was strongly suspected he sold the illicit meat to his unwitting customers. His former good character had been weighed each time prior to sentencing and he had gone free. According to pioneer-historian John McClintock, Keating's indiscretions became intolerable to the vigilantes when he fled out the back door of a competitor's shop while there to sell his oversupply. It was supposed that a rancher who had just entered the shop was, as the old story goes, about to find out how his own beef tasted.[13]

A few days after this hasty departure, on September 18th, a man named Brown discovered the bodies of Davis and Keating "hanging from the limb of a tree in a dark wooded ravine" on Davis' ranch. To those who visited the scene it appeared that they had been caught napping by the vigilantes. Their horses had been unsaddled and their blankets bore every indication of having been "occupied by somebody." Tracks also indicated that they had been given a trial of some sort by six or seven men who then rode toward Spearfish Valley.[14]

Several witnesses were examined by the coroner's jury, which returned the verdict that Davis and Keating had been "hung by parties unknown" and there the matter officially rested. Exactly how Brown happened to be in the area was never satisfactorily explained.

Deadwood restauranter Joe Gandolfo did not overlook the advertising possibilities that a double lynching presented. Gandolfo inserted a card in the **Black Hills Daily Times** which stated: "If horse thieves could always take their last meal before meeting the vigilanters, at Joe Gandolfo's they could 'shuffle off this mortal coil' with the happy consciousness of having reached the highest point of epicurian bliss." A real "rustler," that man Joe Gandolfo![15]

Davis' brother published a card of his own in Deadwood's **Black Hills Pioneer** in which he claimed his brother had gone out to secure some horses he thought Johnson had cached in the vicinity to secure a claim he held against Johnson.[16]

Exactly how the vigilantes got the drop on Keating and Davis was speculative. The most prevalent theory was that "Lengthy" Johnson had cast honesty among thieves aside to save his own neck. Just prior to the double lynching, Johnson had been taken in by a squad of Uncle Sam's blue coats at Camp Bradley (a summer camp on the Little Missouri River, northwest of Deadwood) for admiring some of their mounts a little too closely. He hadn't actually stolen anything before he was cinched, but his reputation had preceded him. It was thought that Johnson, while "in the toils" at Camp Bradley, had written a letter to Keating which induced him to be at Davis' ranch the night of September 18th. Keating, in turn, was known to have talked Davis into accompanying him.[17] In Davis' case, it may have been guilt by association. Those who felt that Johnson was responsible for assisting the vigilantes needed to ask only one question to make their point: If

Johnson hadn't helped the vigilantes, why then, couldn't four prominent citizens of Spearfish Valley be located in an attempt to subpoena them in a stock stealing case against Johnson? Was that his payoff?[18]

General Luther P. Bradley, Commander of 9th Infantry at Ft. Laramie. (*Photo: Courtesy Wyoming State Archives, Museums, and Historical Department.*)

Johnson may have been held at Camp Bradley long enough to help the vigilantes put ropes around two necks, but he still had an overwhelming compulsion to save his own neck. He soon proved that he was more than a match for a whole regiment of blue coats. He bided his time, and when it came, he cut a hole in the rear of his tent and skipped. The first night that he was out on leg bail he walked fifteen miles, into Spearfish, and had the shackles removed from his ankles and wrists. "Lengthy" celebrated on the second night of his regained freedom and returned to Camp Bradley — where he stole the three horses that he was originally after. Under guard at the Camp was the unfortunate corporal who had been assigned to guard Johnson the night that he escaped. For some reason the upper echelons felt that Johnson had received some assistance from within, and that the corporal might be guilty of a little too much complicity. Johnson's conscience, such as it was, allowed him to let the corporal remain where he was.[19]

"Lengthy" soon made his ultimate display of "broad, open frankness," to which he added a touch of exhibitionism. After his performance at Camp Bradley, he went to Central City and was seen frequently on the streets of the upper camps, to converse with his ac-

quaintances, to whom he rehearsed the details of his latest
exploit. Yes, it was even said that
Johnson had a certain amount of
tenacity. It was September 20th,
the same day that most of Central
City had turned out to help Mrs.
George Keating bury her husband.[20]

Tombstone of Orbean Davis, Rose Hill
Cemetery, Spearfish. The location of
George Keating's grave has been lost to
time. (*Author's photo.*)

1. **Black Hills Daily Times,** September 27, 1878. Johnson's exploits
    were chronicled under his various names. It was "Long" Johnson,
    for example, who was captured as reported in the **Black Hills Daily
    Times,** September 20, 1878, but it was "Gus." Johnson whose escape
    was reported in the same paper three days later.
2. **Cheyenne Daily Leader,** September 11, 21, 1878.
3. **Cheyenne Daily Leader,** September 21, 25, 1878.
4. **Cheyenne Daily Leader,** September 25, 26, 1878. The new name for
    the old Red Cloud Agency is the Pine Ridge Reservation. Dee
    Brown, ed., **Bury My Heart at Wounded Knee,** pp. 416-7.
5. Ibid.
6. **Black Hills Daily Times,** October 2, 21, 1878.
7. **Cheyenne Daily Leader,** September 26, 1878; **Black Hills Daily
    times,** October 21, 1878.
8. **Black Hills Daily Times,** October 21, 1878.
9. **Cheyenne Daily Leader,** October 22, 1878; **Black Hills Daily Times,**
    September 30, 1878.
10. **Black Hills Daily Times,** July 16, 1878. Although Annie Tallent, in
    The Black Hills or Last Hunting Grounds of the Dakotahs, pp. 420-1,
    identifies one of the victims as George Skeating, and places the date
    as August, 1877, she does offer one name that may have been the
    "fixed" rustler: Jack Cole.
11. **Black Hills Daily Times,** July 24, 1878.
12. **Black Hills Daily Times,** September 19, 1878.
13. Ibid.; John S. McClintock, **Pioneer Days in the Black Hills,** pp.
    181-2.
14. **Black Hills Daily Times,** September 19, 1878.
15. **Black Hills Daily Times,** September 21, 1878.
16. The **Black Hills Daily Times,** September 25, 1878 issue mentioned
    the card which Davis' brother had printed in the **Pioneer.**
17. **Black Hills Daily Times,** September 19, 20, 1878.
18. **Black Hills Daily Times,** September 16, 1878.
19. **Cheyenne Daily Leader,** September 26, 1878; **Black Hills Daily
    Times,** September 23, 1878.
20. **Black Hills Daily Times,** September 20, 27, 1878.

BIG NOSE GEORGE

A lynch mob and a frontier doctor combined to transform Big Nose George, a notorious outlaw, into a Wyoming legend. Contemporary newspaper accounts, frequently quoted in length, are required to separate the legend from the truth.

The details of Big Nose George's pre-outlaw life remain sketchy. He said he ". . . was born in Indiana, of respectable parents, and while yet a youth, removed to Ottumwa, Iowa. From thence he came west and led a roving life in the mountains . . ."[1] A search of the 1850 Wapello County, Iowa, census reveals that there were two married men with the surname Parrot who lived in the Ottumwa area, either one of whom could have been his father.[2] Prior to his death, Big Nose George stated that he was not yet twenty-nine years old. Therefore, he would not have appeared on the 1850 census.[3]

The only known photograph of Big Nose George was taken in Omaha during his extradition to Wyoming. *(Photo: Courtesy of Union Pacific Railroad Museum.)*

The driving of a bull team over the Cheyenne-Black Hills freight route was probably the only legitimate occupation he pursued in the Black Hills area.[4] After Big Nose George turned road agent he preferred stages traveling on the Sidney route, a possible indication that he pursued the vocation of freighter over the Cheyenne-Black Hills route long enough to become well known to the regular travelers and those who lived along the latter route.

Big Nose George then "joined a gang of horse-thieves and road agents, of which Jack Campbell, Dutch Charlie, Frank Towle and McKinney were members." Through prison sentences and death, Big Nose George eventually reigned as the leader of the outlaw band. At the time of his arrest Big Nose George had been a road agent for three or four years and, it was thought, belonged to the last of the gangs that "used to make a stage trip over the Sidney line so interesting . . ."[5]

His true surname remains as unknown today as it was in 1880, when the **Black Hills Times** reported his arrest: ". . . Big Nose George, whose other name is unknown . . ."[6] Speculation about his "maiden name" includes Parrot, Parrott, Parrotte, Lathrop, Manuse, Curry, Warden, Werner, and Buckley. While not presuming to tell you who he was, the following may be of some help with who he wasn't.

Wild and Woolly: An Encyclopedia of the Old West offers the following mis-information about Big Nose George under the heading George Manuse: "George, whose aliases include 'George Curry', 'George Parrott', and 'Flat-nose George' . . .".[7]

Perhaps a brief look at 'Flat-nose George' is in order. 'Flat-nose George', whose true surname was Currie, was one of the earliest outlaws of the Hole-in-the-Wall and Powder River regions of Wyoming. It was from 'Flat-nose George' that "Kid Curry" learned the finer points of rustling, and from whom he adopted the name Curry, although he was the eldest of four Logan brothers. Although cemetery records indicate that the correct spelling of 'Flat-nose George's' surname was Currie, it too, is often spelled Curry which only adds to the confusion. While Big Nose George may have used the name Curry on occasion, it takes no particular astuteness to doubt that he ever tried to pass himself off as 'Flat-nose George'. From Joe LeFors' posthumous autobiography, **Wyoming Peace Officer**, it is learned that the handle 'Flat-nose George' was well deserved. LeFors recalled that "standing at his side, one could see his eyelids standing higher than the bridge of his nose."[8] Hardly a description that would fit Big Nose George.

Jay Robert Nash's **Bloodletters and Badmen** interweaves the macabre post mortem events that surrounded Big Nose George into the death of 'Flat-nose George'. 'Flat-nose George' was killed by a posse April 17, 1900, near Castle Gate, Utah, and nothing bizarre occurred after his death.[9]

Parrotte, found in some works, William MacLeod Raines', **Guns of the Frontier** being the most notable, is due to the fact that Big Nose George left a French national widow. In 1881 the Governor of Wyoming received from A. Lafaiore, Consul General of France, a request for a death certificate for "... the late George Parrot, alias Au-Groz-Nez . . . The aforesaid certificate of death is required by the widow."[10] Unfortunately, no record of the correspondence was retained by the Consul General's office.[11]

Parrot or Parrott, the second spelling being in general use, is accepted by some as his real surname and dismissed by others as a redundant reference to his nose. Writer Carl Breihan wondered, in 1955, if Big Nose George should not be given credit for thinking of Parrott all on his own. However, by 1960, Mr. Breihan had, "after lengthy research", come to the conclusion that his true surname was Lathrop; as had writer Carelton May in 1958. Neither, however, documented their conclusions.[12]

Lathrop first appeared in **Range Rider**, the autobiography of Robert "Bud" Cowan. Cowan gave a correct account of the killing of Tom Albro, then completely destroyed his credibility with the most incredible account of Big Nose George's arrest to find its way into print. More about both later.[13]

The Great Falls, Montana, **Tribune**, June 30, 1901, tells us that Big Nose George Buckley cast his gaze over the lynch mob and uttered these, his last, words:

> How fain like Pilate would I wash my hands
> Of that most grievous murder, foully done
> But who art thou that hath a holy feeling in my soul
> To consel me to make my peace with God?
> And art thou yet to thine own soul so blind
> That thou wilt war with God by murdering me?[14]

Outlaw Shakespearean? Maybe, but definitely not Big Nose George. Probably wasn't Big Nose George Buckley either.

There was a John Manuese, another outlaw contemporary of Big Nose George's, but no contemporary accounts mention them as being related. Manuese was discharged from the Wyoming Territorial

Penitentiary on December 24, 1881. Manuese had served a two and a half year sentence, which was during Big Nose George's most active period as an outlaw, and eliminates any possibility of their being the same individual.[15]

George Francis Warden is the name Big Nose George gave a Rawlins, Wyoming, reporter during a cell block interview shortly before his death. Werder appeared in a **Miles City Daily Press** interview with one of his defense attorneys, and is probably a corruption of Warden.[16]

Rawlins, Wyoming, the site of the lynching of Big Nose George. (Photo: Courtesy of Union Pacific Railroad Museum.)

From the cell block interview came the most complete description of him by a contemporary. The reporter described Big Nose George as "a man about 35 years old, five feet ten inches tall, rather spare built and will weigh about 160 pounds, dark complexion, black hair and beard, sharp rather piercing eyes and a very prominent nose." He concluded that Big Nose George was "really not as bad a looking fellow as one would expect."[17] By 1902, however, Big Nose George and the legend had begun to grow. A March 16, 1902, **Anaconda Standard** article stated that Big Nose George stood over six feet two, and his face was a "striking index to his character".[18]

The first crime that Big Nose George can definitely be associated with was his most infamous: the attempted a la Jesse James derailment of a Union Pacific train near Elk Mountain, Wyoming. In all probability, the most accurate account of the August 19, 1878, attempt and subsequent movement of the outlaws came from Big Nose George himself. Of his fellow conspirators Frank Towle had been killed by Boone May; "Dutch Charlie" had been lynched at Carbon; and the man who claimed to have been one of the James brothers was reported to have been killed in Montana. The deaths left Big Nose

George alone, in jail "very frightened and depressed." Big Nose
George had nothing to lose, and told the reporter who later wrote it
from memory:

> Our party pulled the spike that held the rail, but our
> crowbar being a short one, we could not pry out the rail. We
> laid in a gully nearby all day and watched the section men at
> work, they not discovering that the rail had been tampered
> with until they were just about to leave . . . Two of our party
> went to Medicine Bow station and purchased provisions.
> After the sectionmen left . . . we again commenced work on
> the rail, and were driven away by the approach of the
> passenger train from the east. When we left we proceeded to
> Elk Mountain. The first we saw of Widdowfield and Vinson
> (sic) they were about a mile off, and we took them to be loose
> horses, but shortly made out that they were men and were
> making direct for our camp . . . it was decided to hide our
> horses in the brush and conceal ourselves and let the men pass
> should they not be officers, and to kill them should they be
> such, as we expected they would say something to give us an
> idea as to who they were.

> They rode up the trail to our camp fire, when the large
> man (Widdowfield) got off of his horse and stuck his hand in-
> to the fire, remarking, "It is as hot as hell; they have been
> here, and we will catch them before long." One of our party
> had a lame horse for which he had been fixing a pair of shoes,
> and Widdowfield picked up the corks which had been cut off,
> saying they were the heads of railroad spikes. Frank Tolle
> (sic), one of our party, then said, "Let's fire," and loud
> enough for all to hear. Part of us shooting at the man on the
> ground and part of us at the man on the horse. I fired at the
> man on the horse. After our volley the horses and rider run
> about fifty yards, when the latter fell off his horse, and at-
> tempted to get up, holding his gun in his hands. Some twenty
> shots were fired at him and the firing ceased when we were
> certain he was dead. Jack Campbell took Widdowfield's
> boots and Dutch Charlie the best saddle. After taking what
> valuables they had, we got scared and did not know what to
> do with the bodies but finally concluded to carry them down
> in the brush and cover them up which we did. We immediate-
> ly broke camp, came down the canyon the way we went up
> and started north. We crossed the railroad at Carbon and the

Platte river about two miles above the mouth of the Muddy. Sim Wan was the leader of the party, he being acquainted with the country. One of the party, called Mack . . . claimed to be one of the James brothers . . .[19]

Carbon, Wyoming, now a ghost town, as it appeared in 1879. *(Photo: Courtesy Union Pacific Railroad Museum.)*

The bodies of Widdowfield and Vincent, who had been told of the pulled spikes, were not found for ten days. Widdowfield was a deputy sheriff stationed at Carbon and "Tip" Vincent was employed

by the Union Pacific Railroad. Big Nose George later said that he could not sleep without seeing the bodies of both dead men.[20] The killing of Widdowfield and Vincent would be a nemesis to all of the men concerned except to Frank James.

Marker placed at the site of the killings of Widdowfield and Vincent. "Robert Widdowfield of Carbon and Tip Vincent of Rawlins, Wyo. Murdered here August 19, 1878. Arrcted by James Fisher Carbon, Wyo. 1892" *(Photo: Courtesy Carbon County Museum.)*

Many writers and historians "credit" Big Nose George with participation in the bold Canyon Springs hold-up of September 28, 1878, near the present Four Corners, Wyoming, in which $27,000 to $40,000 was stolen.[21] **Gold in the Black Hills, Pioneer Days in the Black Hills,** and numerous other accounts identify Big Nose George as the dead outlaw left behind by his comrades. However, the only fatality suffered by the outlaws was one wounded man, who was transported out of the area in a spring wagon. Although no grave could be found, a witness said he had seen a burial take place near Rochford.22

The next crime that Big Nose George can definitely be associated with was the February, 1879, robbery of Morris Cahn. Morris Cahn, former post trader at Ft. Keogh and of late a prospering Miles City merchant, quietly planned a buying trip to the east. Cahn felt a justifiable uneasiness about traveling the first portion of his route, from Miles City to Bismarck, alone. He would be carrying a large amount of money and the land was unsettled and open. Through his former position as post trader, Cahn was able to arrange to accompany an army ambulance, with escort, as far as Bismarck. The escort was not along solely to accommodate Cahn, but to guard the payroll for Ft. Keogh on the return trip. It was near the present Terry, Montana, at a location known as Kahn's Coulee, that Morris Cahn's fortune deserted him, aided and abetted by Big Nose George & Company. The civilian driver of the ambulance later said of the hold-up:

> Reaching the edge of the coulee, I was adjusting myself in the seat, drawing the lines a little more taut as the mules dipped down into the coulee and then straightened up to catch the weight of the wagon, when suddenly I heard the command to stop. I looked sideways and saw a man with a rifle in his hand. The mules might have been frightened a little because they started up at the shout, and it was all I could do to hold them back. The escort wagon was not in sight. I told the fellow I would stop as quickly as I could. We reached the bottom of the coulee before I got the mules stopped. Then I noticed a couple of other fellows, all wearing masks. They saw the wagon coming in the rear and left at once, taking the soldiers unawares and getting them out, marched them down to our wagon, lined us up and searched the men. I didn't understand then, but I did afterwards, why one of gang gave me a cigar. It was Cahn's money they were after. The taking of the small change of the others was only a stall. When they got Cahn's money they were satisfied.23

The gang could well afford the charitable gift of the cigar. They had just relieved Mr. Cahn of $3,200 — not one shot had been fired, nor were any arrests made later for the robbery.

Not long after the robbery of Cahn, Custer County Sheriff Tom Irvine recognized Big Nose George from the reward notices sent out in connection with the deaths of Widdowfield and Vincent. Big Nose George was taken into custody, but a deputy U.S. Marshal who was to make positive identification failed to arrive within the allotted time and Irvine was forced to free his prisoner.[24]

Irvine's efforts were not all in vain, however, for the gang soon moved on to the Sun River country of Montana. It was here, with Big Nose George at the helm of the gang, that their most ambitious undertaking was planned. While members of the gang worked on local ranches, they planned the robbery of an army paymaster. All would probably have gone well had Jack Campbell's liquor-loosened tongue not wagged one night in Johnny Devine's saloon. Soon Devine was on his way to Helena to warn Army authorities of the impending hold-up. When he traveled through Prickly Pear Canyon, Devine was stopped by the gang, already in place and awaiting the paymaster. The price for Devine's safe passage was some whiskey and cigars. For this, the gang lost the payroll. The large escort that was sent with the paymaster experienced no difficulties with the outlaws.[25]

The New York Illustrated Times captioned this, "Four road agents overpower and plunder two officers and seven soldiers near Bismarck, D.T." (*Photo:* **Badmen of the West.**)

Back once again in Wyoming, Big Nose George did not give up on the idea of an army payroll. Big Nose George and "Dutch Charlie" teamed up with Arapahoe Brown, "the James Brothers", and Black

Henry in another attempt on an army payroll. The stages between Medicine Bow and Ft. Fetterman were being robbed with such regularity that the army sought another means of getting the payroll to the fort. It was thought that the best means of getting through with the payroll intact might be with a freight outfit. Slow and vulnerable, the outlaws would surely overlook that which was most obvious. A freighter named Fisher hid the payroll in baking powder tins and flour sacks, and began his journey to Ft. Fetterman. Fisher's outfit received a thorough going over, but the outlaws let him pass when they failed to discover the strongbox they were sure he carried.[26]

It was in a South Pass City saloon that cowboy Tom Albro sat in on his last poker game. Big Nose George, Frank Simms, and Tom Rutledge rounded out the players. Three of Albro's friends, rightfully suspicious of the game, remained at the bar. According to "Bud" Cowan, who worked with Albro, but who was not present:

> Whenever Rutledge would get the deal Albro would lose the pot. So he got to watching Rutledge, and caught him dealing from the bottom of the deck. He called him down for it, and Rutledge jumped up and called Albro a damned liar and started to pull his gun.

> Albro pulled his gun and shot Rutledge . . . Big Nose George was sitting at Albro's right and he pulled his gun and shot Albro . . . Both were killed instantly.[27]

As Big Nose George rode away, Albro's friends fired some shots at him, but their efforts to follow him were hampered by darkness.

Big Nose George next appeared in the Fort McKinney vicinity where he committed one of his last lawless acts. He and a man reported to have been Carey, but who no doubt was his old sidekick Jack Campbell, rifled old man Hill's camp near Deep Creek. Old man Hill made no resistance as one man held a gun on him, while the other raided his larder of some two hundred pounds of food.[28]

Perhaps it was because they had hit upon hard times, as evidenced by their theft of food, that they returned to Miles City, where crime had once paid Big Nose George well. The fact that Tom Irvine was still sheriff there did not deter them, nor did the fact that rewards totaled $2,000 for Big Nose George and $1,000 for Jack Campbell.[29]

Big Nose George and Campbell arrived, as Sheriff Irvine had been told they would, with a string of stolen horses. In anticipation of their arrival, Irvine had deputized two trusted men, Lem Wilson and Fred Schmalsle, to make the arrest. After they arrived, Big Nose

George sequestered himself in saloonman John Chinnick's cabin, but Jack Campbell allowed himself the freedom of the town. Ironically, Big Nose George was the first to be arrested:

> The day before tackling George, Schmalsle and Wilson, under the pretext of wanting horses, interviewed him and became acquainted. The next night, at dark, they proceeded to where George was staying and leisurely sidled up to their victim who was sitting in the doorway and, in expressive words, Fred told him to throw up, placing a pistol to his left ear. George quickly obeyed, accompanying the action with an exclamation of surprise. They then arrested Carey (sic) in a saloon who, when ordered up, made a motion for his pistol, but changed his mind as he saw the hammer of Fred's self-cocker slowly rise.[30]

Although **The Frontier Years,** based on a manuscript written by Miles City photographer L. A. Huffman, placed "X." Biedler as the arresting officer, replete with the jovial, but deadly Biedler's musings, "X." was nowhere around. **The Yellowstone Journal** clarified Biedler's involvement with the report that, ". . . a day or two after the arrest, X. Biedler arrived having trailed the prisoners to this place . . ."[31]

Sheriff Irvine put Big Nose George in jail and telegraphed Carbon County Sheriff Jim Rankin that he had Big Nose George in custody. Rankin arrived, accompanied by Prosecuting Attorney Smith, and was given custody of Big Nose George who was manacled hand and foot. At some point, either before they left Miles City or en route to Rawlins via Bismarck and Omaha, Jack Campbell either escaped or was freed. It was during a stopover in Omaha that the only known photograph of Big Nose George was taken. In Cheyenne, several local law officers thought they recognized Big Nose George, but no one was positive enough to link him to any other crimes. The next day they resumed their journey to Carbon.[32]

As the train neared Carbon, Rankin recalled the fate of "Dutch Charlie" and gave the handcuff keys to Smith, who sat apart from them. "Dutch Charlie" had been arrested for the murders of Widdowfield and Vincent two years earlier. As the train he was aboard stopped at Carbon, the hometown of Widdowfield . . .

> . . . Last night at 9:25 o'clock, when passenger train No. 3 stopped at this station, a party of masked men . . . broke open the door of the baggage car and took Chas. Bates, alias

"Dutch Charlie", out and hung him to a telegraph pole . . .
Dutch Charlie, just before he was hung, confessed his guilt.[33]

"Dutch Charlie" was game to the very end, and deprived the lynch mob the satisfaction of naming anyone else connected with the murders of Widdowfield and Vincent. His body was cut down the next day and thrown in a Rawlins bound coal car, his newly acquired necktie still around his neck.[34]

As the train pulled into Carbon, Rankin noticed that the stores were lighted and a dance was in progress. As the train came to a stop, the Carbonites began the execution of a well formulated plan. One party secured the engineer and fireman; another "invited" the conductor into the express car. The car occupied by Rankin and his prisoner was then entered by the main party, who proceeded with the business at hand. One man held Rankin, while another searched him for the key to the handcuffs. Unable to find them, one of the band went in search of a sledgehammer. Big Nose George grabbed the revolver of one of the men, but his hands were bound so tightly that he was overpowered before he could fire it. The sledgehammer arrived, and the seat Big Nose George occupied was shattered. A rope was thrown around his neck and he was dragged outside. The Carbonites threw the rope around a corral beam and strung Big Nose George up until he expressed a willingness to confess. After the confession he was taken back and delivered to Rankin. No one appeared to be more impressed by the whole proceedings than a lady from the east who exclaimed, "If I ever get back to Pennsylvany alive I'll never leave it again."[35]

The train, delayed about a half an hour, reached Rawlins near the usual time. Big Nose George was jailed without further incident.

Big Nose George was indicted for murder during the September, 1880, term of court and entered a plea of guilty. Presiding Judge Jacob B. Blair refused his plea and remanded him back to jail to think it over. As Big Nose George was taken from the courtroom, Judge Blair called John W. Meldrum, Clerk of the Second Judicial District, to the bench. Blair to Meldrum, "I want you to go to the jail and interview the gentleman with the pronounced proboscis and ascertain whether or not he is compos mentis."[36]

Meldrum found Big Nose George sitting on the edge of his bunk with his head in his hands. Big Nose George told Meldrum that he was afraid, should he enter a not guilty plea, he would be taken from the jail and lynched by a mob. After Meldrum assured him that would not be the case, he entered a not guilty plea. "I've made up my mind," he told Meldrum, "that this thing is going to cost me my life, and I would rather be hung by the sheriff than by a mob."[37]

After the trial began, Judge William Ware Peck announced that he was satisfied Big Nose George had entered his guilty plea out of a sense of guilt and that to continue the trial would be useless.[38] Judge Peck then called in the Governor of the Wyoming Territory, city and county officials, and all members of the clergy. All were directed to stand at attention as Judge Peck sentenced Big Nose George to death.[39] Big Nose George completely broke down and had to be supported by two deputy sheriffs when the death sentence was pronounced.[40]

Judge Jacob B. Blair refused Big Nose George's "guilty" plea. (Photo: Courtesy Wyoming State Archives, Museums, and Historical Department.)

Judge William Ware Peck sentenced Big Nose George to hang. (Photo: Courtesy Wyoming State Archives, Museums, and Historical Department.)

Big Nose George was remanded to jail and went on a hunger strike. He would not allow himself to be reduced to a skeleton, however, and ended the hunger strike. The hunger strike was soon followed by an escape attempt. A "Special to the Leader," dateline Rawlins, March 22, 1881, told of Big Nose George's attempted escape, and forecast with amazing accuracy the events which were soon to follow:

At 7:30 this evening, when jailor Robert Rankin entered the jail corridor . . . he was attacked by Big Nose George . . . who (had) removed the shackles . . . (and used) them for a weapon, (striking) . . . Rankin over the head . . . severely cutting him. Mrs. Rankin . . . rushed to her husband's rescue, and locking the door . . . (got) a revolver while a sister of Mr. Rankin ran downtown to raise the alarm . . . There is intense excitement in town tonight, and strong talk of lynching . . . extra guards have been taken to prevent an escape.[41]

The extra guards were well equipped to handle another attack from within, but not the mob which appeared at the door of the jail at 10:55 that night. Big Nose George's greatest fear, that of being lynched by a mob, was about to be realized.

Mrs. Rosa Rankin was presented a beautiful gold watch and key in a velvet lined case for preventing the escape of Big Nose George. Mrs. Rosa Rankin was the wife of jailor Robert Rankin and a sister-in-law of Carbon County Sheriff Jeff Rankin. (*Photo: Courtesy Carbon County Museum, Rawlins, Wyoming.*)

Big Nose George was taken outside, where a half-inch rope was tossed over a telegraph pole, and Big Nose George was ordered to stand on an empty kerosene barrel. When the barrel was kicked out from under him the untested rope choked him a little, then broke. Big Nose George was sent sprawling to the ground and begged to be shot instead of lynched. Soon a twelve foot ladder was brought to the scene and he was ordered to climb it. Just before the ladder was pulled away, Big Nose George told the mob, "I will jump off, boys, and break my neck." As the ladder was pulled away Big Nose George lunged for the telegraph pole. While he was cowering on the ground, imploring the mob to shoot him, he had managed to untie his wrists. Three times his strength enabled him to pull himself up before the weight of the shackles, and his own weight, drained his strength. His hands lost their life-saving grip and Big Nose George died, not from the broken neck he had prophesied, but from strangulation.[42]

While the story of most vigilante hangings would end here, the story of Big Nose George does not. It, and he, became a Wyoming legend.

Above: Artists conception of the lynching of Big Nose George, drawn from a description of the affair given by a witness. *(Photo: Courtesy of Wyoming State Archives, Museums, and Historical Department.)*

Left: Photograph of a bullet said to have been removed from the body of Big Nose George. *(Photo: Courtesy of Wyoming State Archives, Museums, and Historical Department.)*

There had arrived in Rawlins a few months earlier a young doctor from Vermont, Dr. John E. Osborne. While the mob had been removing Big Nose George from the jail, three others had gone on a search for Dr. Osborne. When Dr. Osborne refused to comply with their wish that he would pronounce Big Nose George the late Big Nose George, they sent Big Nose George back up the telegraph pole for a second, longer, time. A day passed before he was taken down this time. Several passenger trains stopped; the passengers afforded the opportunity to gaze upon the outcome of a life of lawlessness, much the same as they had when "Dutch Charlie" served as the bad example.[43]

To Coroner Edgerton fell the duty of cutting the body down. Edgerton was followed to Daley's Undertaking Parlor by Dr. Osborne who viewed the lynching as an excellent opportunity to examine the criminal mind, and inquired if he might do just that. Dr. Osborne's examination resulted in the, not altogether surprising, proclamation that the deceased was "not very bright" and another request. Could he make a plaster of Paris death mask of the dead outlaw? His second request was granted and the top of Big Nose George's skull was put back in place, more or less, and the death mask was made. Dr. Osborne was next permitted to remove some skin from the deceased's thighs and chest. Dr. Osborne used some of the skin, which he had tanned, as "trim" for his medicine bag, but the majority of it went into the making of a pair of shoes. Osborne later complained, "I instructed the shoemaker to keep the nipples on the skin . . . but he did not follow my instructions."[44]

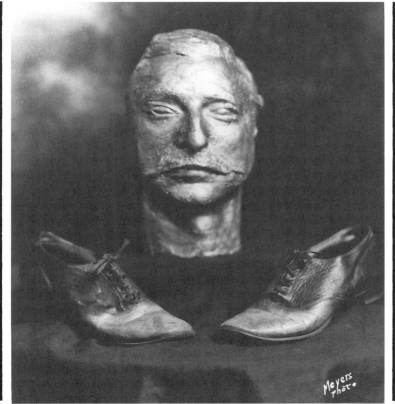

Death mask and shoes made from the skin of Big Nose George. *(Photo: Courtesy Wyoming State Archives, Museums, and Historical Dept.)*

Manacles, death mask, and piece of tanned skin. *(Photo: Courtesy Union Pacific Railroad Museum.)*

To his assistant, Dr. Lillian Heath, Dr. Osborne presented the skull cap in lieu of a piece of the tanned skin. Dr. Heath had taken no part in Dr. Osborne's bizarre experiments, but was his assistant in his medical practice only.[45]

Dr. John Osborne, Rawlins physician.
(*Photo: Courtesy Wyoming State Archives, Museums and Historical Department.*)

The body of Big Nose George was finally put in a whiskey barrel, with a bottle of Lydia Pinkham's Vegetable Compound, and buried.

In 1950 workmen digging the foundation for a Rawlins business unearthed a wooden barrel which was found to contain a skeleton. Someone at the scene recalled the story of Big Nose George and inquired if Dr. Heath still possessed the skull cap. She did; it was being used as a door-stop in her home. It was taken to the scene, and the match was so perfect that the county coroner declined the joking suggestion that an inquest ought to be held.[46]

The barrel and skeleton as found in Rawlins, Wyoming, May 11, 1950. (*Photo: Courtesy Union Pacific Railroad Museum.*)

Dr. Lillian Heath, as she appeared about the time of the lynching of Big Nose George, and holding the skull cap after the skeleton of Big Nose George was found in 1950. (*Photos: Left, Courtesy Carbon County Museum; Right, Wyoming State Archives, Museums and Historical Dept.*)

The Carbon County Museum was offered the skeleton and declined. The museum's curator, and the man to whom the skeleton was given for disposal, have both since died. There is no clue to the location of the last remains of Big Nose George, the outlaw, who became a pair of shoes and a Wyoming legend.[47]

And what became of Dr. Osborne? He became Governor of Wyoming in 1893.

1.   **Miles City Press,** Miles City, Montana, November 18, 1882.

2.   1850 Wapello County, Iowa, census, District 13, dwelling #1261 occupied by George Parrott, farmer, married, and George Parrott, single, aged 22. Dwelling #1262 occupied by Henry Parrott, married, age 26.

3.   **Cheyenne Daily Leader,** September 15, 1880.

4.   **Black Hills Daily Times,** July 27, 1880.

5.   Ibid.

6.   Ibid.

7.   Dennis McLoughlin, **Wild and Woolly; An Encyclopedia of the Old West,** p. 324.

8.   Dorothy M. Johnson, "Durable Desperado Kid Curry", **Montana, Magazine** of Western History, Vol. 6, No. 2, p. 24; Joe LeFors, **Wyoming Peace Officer,** p. 103; Flat-nose George was killed by a posse near Castle Gate, Utah, April 17, 1900. Cemetery records indicate Currie was the correct spelling. Flat-nose George is buried at Chadron, Nebraska.

9.   Jay Robert Nash, **Bloodletters and Badmen,** p. 612. Readable, but unreliable where the outlaws of this area are concerned. Follows many of the legends, such as Tom Horn being hanged with a rope he himself braided.

10.   **Cheyenne Daily Leader,** August 20, 1881; William MacLeod Raine, **Guns of the Frontier,** pp. 121-122.

11.   Jean Thebrand, Deputy Consul, Consulate General de France, New York City, New York to author, June 27, 1979.

12.   Carl Breihan, "Big Nose George", **Westerners Brand Book,** (New York Posse, Vol. 2, No. 2), 1955, p. 36; Carelton May, "Big Nose George", **Real West,** Winter Issue, 1958.

13.   Robert Ellsworth "Bud" Cowan, **Range Rider,** pp. 92-106. Cowan gives us Sheriff Rankin, disguised as a trapper, going into the mountains. In the mountains he builds a cabin, traps all winter and forms the acquaintance of Big Nose George. During the winter Big Nose George got to know, and trust, Rankin. Then, after a monumental drinking bout, Big Nose George awakens from a slumber and finds he is handcuffed fore and aft to the bed.

14.   **Great Falls Tribune,** Great Falls, Montana, June 30, 1901.

15.   Wyoming State Archives and Historical Department, Cheyenne, Wyoming, to author, March 28 and June 29, 1979.

16.   **Miles City Daily Press,** November 18, 1882.

17.   **Cheyenne Daily Sun,** August 17, 1880.

18.   **Anaconda Standard,** Anaconda, Montana, March 16, 1902. This description also appeared in a nearly verbatim article in the **Judith Gap Journal,** January 1, 1924.

19.   The James Gang is credited with the July 21, 1873, robbery of a train near Adair, Iowa, in which the spikes had been pulled. **History of Adair County,** Iowa, p. 217; **Cheyenne Daily Sun,** August 17, 1880.

20.   **Cheyenne Daily Leader,** September 15, 1880.

21.   Watson Parker, **Gold in the Black Hills,** fixes the amount at $27,000 (p. 176) while John McClintock's **Pioneer Days in the Black Hills** puts the amount at $40,000 (p. 214).

22.   **Black Hills Daily Times,** November 8, 1878; Agnes Wright Spring, **The Cheyenne and Black Hills Stage and Express Routes,** p. 272.

23. The Yellowstone Journal, August 7, 1880, fixes the date of the robbery as February, 1879; The Judith Basin Press, March 6, 1933; Cahn was appointed post trader in July, 1877. History of Montana, 1739-1885, p. 1036.

24. Black Hills Daily Times, July 27, 1880.

25. Anaconda Standard, March 16, 1902.

26. Annals of Wyoming, April, 1958, Vol. 30, No. 1, p. 35.

27. Robert Ellsworth "Bud" Cowan, op. cit., p. 93.

28. Yellowstone Journal, August 7, 1880.

29. Cheyenne Daily Leader, July 20, 1880, identifies the outlaws as Big Nose Jim and Jack Campbell. Black Hills Daily Times, July 27, 1880, also states Jack Campbell. Yellowstone Journal, August 7, 1880, the source of the quote, states most of the reward money was consumed by expenses in guarding and jailing the prisoners.

30. Yellowstone Journal, August 7, 1880.

31. Ibid.; Brown and Felton, The Frontier Years, pp. 156-158.

32. Cheyenne Daily Leader, July 20, 1880; The Black Hills Journal, January 5, 1878, states "by a slight miscalculation Jack Campbell escaped . . ." This is the arrest before the gang went to the Sun River country. Of the last arrest, The Yellowstone Journal, August 7, 1880, stated, "heavily chained together, they were taken away . . ."; M. Wilson Rankin, Reminiscences of Frontier Days, p. 109, details the route taken.

33. Cheyenne Daily Leader, January 7, 1879.

34. Ibid.; Rankin, op. cit.

35. Cheyenne Daily Sun, August 11, 1880.

36. John W. Meldrum, "The Taming of 'Big Nose George' - and Others", The Union Pacific Magazine, November, 1926, p. 8-9.

37. Ibid.

38. Cheyenne Daily Leader, November 20, 1880.

39. Cheyenne Daily Leader, December 18, 1880; Meldrum, op. cit.

40. Cheyenne Daily Leader, December 18, 1880.

41. Cheyenne Daily Leader, March 31, 1881.

42. Cheyenne Daily Leader, March 31, 1881; Miles City Daily Press, November 18, 1882.

43. M. Wilson Rankin, op. cit.; Rawlins Republican and Wyoming Reporter, June 9, 1927.

44. Ibid.; Rawlins Daily Times, May 12, 1950; Dabney Otis Collins, "Skin Game in Wyoming", Empire Magazine, November 17, 1974, p. 31.

45. Mrs. Bess Sheller, County Librarian, Carbon County Public Library, to author, November 5, 1979.

46. Rawlins Daily Times, May 12, 1950.

47. Sheller, op. cit.

CURLY GRIMES

William Henry Harrison Llewellyn of Omaha, Nebraska, was appointed a special agent for the Department of Justice about June 1, 1879. Llewellyn's first assignment as a special agent was to capture and arrest persons stealing Indian ponies in Dakota Territory and Nebraska.[1] To the residents of the area where Llewellyn concentrated his efforts, mid to southeastern Dakota into mid and northeastern Nebraska, the assignment translated stop "Doc" Middleton. Middleton, Nebraska's premier horse thief, was at the height of his career when

William Henry Harrison Llewellyn. *(Photo: Courtesy Museum of New Mexico.)*

"Doc" Middleton. *(Photo: Courtesy Nebraska State Historical Society.)*

Llewellyn became a special agent. Whether real or implied, the assignment resulted in the arrest of Middleton on July 27, 1879.[2] After Middleton's arrest, Llewellyn's case load was expanded to include investigation of other federal crimes such as the robbery of the Bone Creek, Nebraska, post office.

On July 5, 1879 two Middleton satellites, Joe Johnson and Jack Nolan, combined in the robbery with a former stage driver who had said he was going to the Black Hills to "make a raise" by robbing stagecoaches. The trio threatened postmaster Ed Cook with death should he report the broad daylight robbery. Cook was familiar with the time that the same trio had robbed a deputy sheriff of his horse, gun, and money near Atkinson, Nebraska, and remained silent. The deputy had gone out to arrest Nolan for the murder of a Mexican cowboy at Sidney, and was sent back to town carrying his saddle. Due to Cook's silence, warrants were not issued for Nolan and Johnson until October 9 when the robbery became common knowledge. It was from Nolan and Johnson that Llewellyn learned Curly Grimes was the third man — not from postmaster Ed Cook.[3]

Chief Postal Inspector John B. Furay advised Llewellyn to look up Boone May and take him along "for safety" before he went out after Grimes. Grimes, known variously as William Curley, Lew Curley, and Lee Curley was known to be a dangerous man with a gun. He had perfected a method of "fanning" his revolvers which made him one of the fastest shooters in the territory — some claimed west of the Missouri. Those who had been privileged to witness Grimes' dexterity and marksmanship said that he could put every bullet into an oyster can at one hundred yards if he took his time and didn't "fan" his weapons.[4]

> It was claimed "by those who ought to know that Curly has committed more than one murder in addition to the two Missourians who visited the Niobrara Valley last year (1879) to purchase farms. He fell out with Doc Middleton because that bandit deemed him too bad to belong to his gang of horse thieves and cutthroats." A letter, signed "Fair Play," to the editor of the **Black Hills Daily Times** stated that Curly had been arrested for the Bone Creek post office robbery, "and broke jail."

Llewellyn learned that Grimes was "on the road" with Morris Appel's freight outfit and sought out Boone May. They requisitioned horses from Ft. Meade and began their pursuit. The bull train was located on Elk Creek, thirty-five miles out of Deadwood, and the unarmed Grimes was arrested without incident. Although Grimes had earlier expressed a great fear of being arrested by Llewellyn, his only

comment after the warrant was read was to say, "You are Llewellyn."
It was -20° out and Grimes complained that his hands would freeze if
the handcuffs were not removed. He promised not to attempt to
escape, and they were removed. They were seen by several persons as

they returned to Ft. Meade, but
always at a distance so no one except May and Llewellyn could re-
late what occurred after they
were out of the freighter's camp.[5]

Morris Appel, pioneer freighter and charter member of the Black Hills Stock Association. *(Photo: Courtesy South Dakota State Historical Society.)*

They arrived at Erb's Bull Dog Ranch about seven hours after the
arrest. It was there that Grimes gave the first indication that he wasn't
as complacent about his arrest as he first appeared. Grimes, riding in
the lead, stooped down and picked up a sled stake from the ground as
he rode around the corner of the house. Llewellyn's eye caught the un-
natural movement and he trained his shotgun on Grimes. Grimes
raised his hands and the intended weapon fell harmlessly to the
ground.[6]

About two miles from the Bull Dog Ranch, Grimes made his
brief, fatal ride for freedom. It was between nine and ten o'clock at
night; a blinding blizzard obliterated all nearby landmarks. Grimes
was some twenty feet ahead of his captors when he looked back, turned around, and dug his spurs into his little Texas pony. He heard the
command to halt . . . Llewellyn . . . a shotgun blast . . . shot flying
overhead . . . another, something pierced his saddle . . . tore into his
back . . . another shot . . . hit, hit bad . . . falling out of the saddle . . .
foot's caught . . . the ground's coming . . . he lost consciousness . . .[7]

Grimes was dead by the time Llewellyn and May reached him.
They left him much as he fell, his hat drawn over his face, his riding

whip across his arms, and continued to Ft. Meade. Upon their arrival they informed Lt. Scott that Grimes had been killed when he attempted to escape. It was February 3, 1880. The coroner was summoned from Deadwood, but a question of jurisdiction arose and it was not until February 11 that an inquest was held. By that time the body of Grimes had been buried by a detail dispatched from Ft. Meade. The inquest was of little consequence; Curly Grimes had come to his death from shots fired by Boone May and William H. H. Llewellyn.[8]

The unmarked grave of Curly Grimes, the man some thought was the fastest shooter west of the Missouri. The grave is off I-90 near the National Cemetery. *(Author's photo.)*

Many factors led to the arrests of May and Llewellyn for the murder of Curly Grimes. The fact that Boone May was present prejudiced some opinions. Others felt that Llewellyn had attempted to assassinate "Doc" Middleton, and while not able to do so, had not given up on the idea. Despite Llewellyn's assurances to his superiors that he **wanted** to be tried so he could be cleared of any wrongdoing, one of the predominate reasons was that it had occurred on a military reservation. Grimes' friends did their part to fan the fires of discontent about his death also. The **Cheyenne Daily Leader** bitterly complained that "the citizens of Sturgis and that vicinity are a little too fast in the matter of condeming Boone May and Detective Llewellyn for the killing of Curley (sic), the reputed road agent. The people want to see every bandit in the country fixed, but as soon as one is planted in any particular locality the people . . . generally succeed in creating sympathy for the dead robber."[9]

Ft. Meade

It was at Ft. Meade, on the parade grounds in the foreground, that the playing of "The Star Spangled Banner" was initiated by Colonel Carlton. Played at all band practices and functions, the practice spread until 1932 when it became the National Anthem. *(Photo: Courtesy South Dakota Travel Commission.)*

At their hearing Judge Campbell set bail at $10,000 each. To guarantee their appearance, men who represented over $500,000 signed their bonds.[10]

The death of Curly Grimes had one unexpected result that did not set well with Boone May — May, for probably the first time in his life, became the hunted instead of the hunter. Eight of Grimes' avengers stopped a Sidney bound coach and inquired if, perhaps, Boone May was aboard. After they had determined to their satisfaction that he wasn't, the coach was allowed to proceed. Had they stopped the Deadwood bound coach, they would have found the fearless outlaw hunter. As it happened, however, upon the two coaches meeting, Boone May simply changed stages and returned to Sidney. His absence from Deadwood, newsworthy as it was, was not mentioned until he was prepared to return and "get down to cases" with Grimes' avengers. It may have just been a coincidence that his preparations were finalized at the same time he was required to return to Deadwood for the hearing — then again, maybe it wasn't.[11]

Boone May did not spend his time awaiting trial among the idle unemployed. He spent part of the time as a messenger for the Black Hills Placer Mining Company: Ambrose Bierce, Rockerville, General Agent. When Bierce's eastern board of directors expressed their displeasure with Bierce for hiring a man under indictment for murder the fiesty Bierce placed May on the payroll as "Boone May — Murderer."[12]

Bierce, one of two men on the contemporary literary scene to write of Boone May's exploits, did not enlarge upon them to the extent Edgar Beecher Bronson did. "Bitter Bierce," a macabre little man who was rumored to write his best with a skull, a loaded revolver, and the ashes of his deceased son upon his desk, wrote only once of the unpleasant time he had spent in the Black Hills. Boone May figured prominently in "A Sole Survivor," a short story collection of instances in which Bierce was the sole survivor of past gatherings of two or more individuals.[13] Bierce wrote:

> I knew the road fairly well, for I had previously traveled it by night, on horseback, my pockets bulging with currency and my free hand holding a cocked revolver the entire distance of fifty miles. To make the journey by wagon with a companion (Boone May) was a luxury. Still, the drizzle of the rain was uncomfortable. May sat hunched up beside me, a rubber poncho over his shoulders and a Winchester rifle in its leathern case between his knees. I thought him a trifle off his guard, but said nothing. The road, barely visible, was rocky, the wagon rattled, and alongside ran a roaring stream. Suddenly we heard through it all, the clinking of a horse's shoes directly behind, and simultaneously the short, sharp words of authority: "Throw up your hands."
>
> With an involuntary jerk at the reins I brought my team to its haunches and reached for my revolver. Quite needless: with the quickest movement that I had ever seen in anything but a cat — almost before the words were out of the horseman's mouth — May had thrown himself backward across the back of the seat, face upward, and the muzzle of his rifle was within a yard of the fellow's breast! What further occurred among the three of us there in the gloom of the forest has, I fancy, never been accurately related.[14]

The 1914 disappearance of Ambrose Bierce, "Bitter Bierce," to his detractors, ranks as one of the most mysterious in North America. Bierce disappeared in Mexico. *(Photo: Courtesy Huntington Library.)*

The very nature of "A Sole Survivor" dictates that Boone May, while under indictment for the murder of Curly Grimes, dispensed yet another outlaw to push clouds against the sky.

Llewellyn and May were tried August 23, 1880 at Deadwood. The defense strategy was simple: a parade of witnesses attesting to the totally unacceptable nature of the deceased, Curly Grimes. His use of aliases, how he had said he planned to "make a raise," his shooting ability, and the fact that he sometimes dyed his light mustache dark in contrast to his shoulder length blonde hair came under discussion. Llewellyn testified that the jaded government horses he and May rode would have been no match for Grimes' little pony, but did not expound on their use of long range wire bullets to stop Grimes. Boone May did not give any testimony that had not been given previously, but simply supported Llewellyn's testimony. Boone was like that under pressure; quick on the trigger, but not much given to talk. The only man who could have refuted any on the testimony was the late Curly Grimes.[15]

The gravesite of Curly Grimes. Sign, no longer standing, incorrectly dated the date of Grimes' death. *(Photo: Courtesy S.D. Division of Tourism.)*

Despite a recent court ruling that shooting a prisoner was justifiable only when the prisoner was under arrest for a felony and had threatened the officer's life, the jury returned a not guilty verdict. The crowded courtroom rang with applause when the verdict was announced. The jury had not left the jury box.[16]

Llewellyn remained a special agent of the Department of Justice until November 30, 1880. Among the first of the many political plums Llewellyn reaped was appointment as agent to the Mescalaro and Apache reservations. Llewellyn served in the Rough Riders in Cuba where he became acquainted with Teddy Roosevelt, who later appointed him the District Attorney for Southern New Mexico. He also served as Attorney for the Territory of New Mexico during the years 1905-1907. One man that knew Roosevelt and Llewellyn said, "I think the President thought more of Llewellyn than of any other man in New Mexico." On June 11, 1927 Llewellyn died in El Paso, Texas. He had outlived his old foe, "Doc" Middleton, by fourteen years.[17]

1.   Letter, Ferris, E. Stovel, Judicial and Fiscal Branch, Civil Archives Division, National Archives and Records Service, Washington, D.C., to author, February 1, 1979.
2.   For information about the arrest of Middleton, see Harold Hutton, **Doc Middleton**, pp. 113-128.
3.   **Black Hills Daily Times,** August 24, 1880; Hutton, pp. 74, 91, and 111. Willard and Brown, **The Black Hills Trails,** pp. 274-276.
4.   **Black Hills Daily Times,** op. cit.
*   **Black Hills Daily Times,** February 15, 1880.
5.   Ibid.
6.   Ibid.
7.   Ibid.
8.   Ibid.; Undated article in author's files.
9.   **Cheyenne Daily Leader,** February 19, 1880; **Black Hills Daily Times,** op. cit.; William H. H. Llewellyn to Hon. Charles Devans, Attorney General, Washington, D.C. Record Group 60, National Archives and Records Service.
10.   **Deadwood Pioneer,** August 22, 1880.
11.   **Black Hills Daily Times,** March 17, 1880.
12.   Paul Fatout, **Ambrose Bierce and the Black Hills,** pp. 76-77.
13.   Ibid.; Ambrose Bierce, "A Sole Survivor", a short story from **The Collected Works of Ambrose Bierce.** Whether Bierce actually wrote under these conditions or not is not known. As evidenced by the portrait, he certainly did nothing to dispel the story.
14.   **The Collected Work of Ambrose Bierce,** op. cit.
15.   **Black Hills Daily Times,** op. cit.
16.   Ibid.; Spring, **The Cheyenne and Black Hills Stage and Express Routes,** pp. 300-301; **Cheyenne Daily Leader,** February 29, 1880.
17.   Stovel to author, op. cit.; H. B. Hening, ed., **George Curry 1861-1947,** p. 209; Hutton, op. cit., p. 211; **Santa Fe New Mexican,** June 13, 1927.

A PRICE ON FRANK TOWLE'S HEAD

Admittedly, the road agents weren't the fashion plates of the Black Hills, but few were in such need of repairs to their attire as those encountered by S. M. Booth in Red Canyon near Custer, September 11, 1878: "The robbers took his shirt studs, cuff buttons, collar button, and even his boots, leaving him barefooted."[1] Pioneer newshound R. B. Hughes felt that Charles Carey, the leader of the Canyon Springs robbers, had stolen Booth's boots. Hughes added that the robber apologized for stealing the boots, but said that it was seldom when he found a pair that fit.[2] Booth, accompanied by D. K. Snively who was also robbed, was forced to return to Custer to re-outfit. In addition to the loss of apparel, Booth lost his team, $1,200 and his provisions. After "going through" the pair, the three robbers bid Mr. Booth "a very cordial adieu" and told him that he could "whack up" with them if he desired. Snively continued on to Cheyenne after the robbery, depending upon the "tender mercies" of incoming freighters to see him through. Later in the day the same trio robbed two telegraph workers of their money, firearms, and watches. They, too, were forced to re-outfit in Custer.[3]

Two nights later Booth's benefactors were joined by another trio in stopping both coaches four miles south of Lance Creek:

> There were two passengers in this coach (the "up" coach), Mr. J. Goldsworthy and Mrs. A. J. Rigby. The thieves took $10 from Mr. Goldsworthy but gave it back again.[4] Nothing was taken from Mrs. Rigby. The thieves then

went through the mail and treasure box and having finished this work let this coach and passengers go on. When the south bound coach reached this spot, it was also stopped. There were two passengers in this coach and two messengers following about two hundred yards behind on horseback. As soon as the coach was halted the messengers dismounted and approached within about fifteen steps of the thieves, one of whom called to the messengers to halt, accompanying his command with a shot. One of the messengers returned the shot, killing the thief, who had just fired, dead. The remaining thieves at this moment began firing at the messengers and retreating towards a gulch close by, to which point the messengers could not follow. The coach, in the meantime, had been ordered to go ahead by the thieves, who had succeeded in robbing one passenger and secured the mail sacks before the fighting began . . .[5]

The messengers, Boone May and John Zimmerman, remained behind for about thirty minutes, but could not dislodge the road agents or reach the mail sacks. Attempts to locate the grave of the dead outlaw proved fruitless, and the **Black Hills Daily Times** questioned if one had been killed.

In late December, John Irwin was arrested in Cheyenne for firing his revolver in McDaniels' Theater. Irwin was suspected of belonging to a gang officers had recently taken in at Rock Creek, and was taken

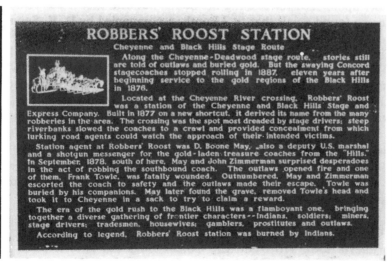

Historic marker near the site of Robbers' Roost station. *(Author's photo.)*

to Laramie. There he admitted to Sheriff N. K. Boswell that he was one of the September 13th robbers. Irwin identified the dead robber as the badly wanted Frank Towle, and gave Boswell directions to his grave. In addition to Irwin and Towle, others identified as participants in the robbery were Frank James, Joe Manuse, and probably Charles Carey. Joe Manuse, one of the men taken in at Rock Creek had the overcoat Boone May lost the night of September 13 in his possession.[6]

Sheriff N. K. Boswell gave Boone May the information that led to one of his most chronicled exploits. *(Photo: Courtesy Wyoming State Archives, Museums, and Historical Department.)*

Boswell relayed the information about Frank Towle's grave to
Boone May, who went to the designated site. There he found Towle's
body and disinterred it. In reporting what happened after that, the
Black Hills Daily Times stated: "There is an inexpressible ghastliness
in the business of carrying a dead road agent's head around in a box
trying to get a bounty on it," but that's what Boone did. With Towle's
head in the box, he rode hard and fast for Cheyenne to claim the $200
Laramie County had offered for each dead or alive road agent. When
the Laramie County Commissioners said they felt they wouldn't be
able to identify Frank Towle "as presented," Boone carried his
trophy to Carbon County in an attempt to collect the reward offered
for the murderers of Widdowfield and Vincent.[7] May supported his
claim to the reward with an affidavit:

Territory of Wyoming

Carbon County, Wyo. T. To Boon May, Dr.
For reward of Frank Toll one of the Murderers of Widdowfield and Vincent

Territory of Wyoming, County of Albany
   Boon May being duly sworn on oath says: That on the
night of 13th of September A.D. 1878 he shot and killed
Frank Toll one of the murderers of Widdowfield and Vincent on the Old Womans fork on the Black Hills Stage road
running from Cheyenne to Deadwood that affiant has the
head of the said Frank Toll in his possession sufficient to
identify him and that affiant is prepared to prove that the
man killed by him as above stated is the identical Frank Toll
and the murderer of Widdowfield at Elk Mountain in said
Carbon County.

Subscribed and sworn to before me this 29th day of January
A.D. 1879

(Seal)   John D. Brockway, Notary
                                                    Public

Carbon County records do not indicate that the reward was ever paid. Up until the time of Big Nose George's confession, there was no actual proof that Frank Towle had been at Elk Mountain. By the time of his confession, the reward had been withdrawn.[8]

On March 5, 1879 the Laramie County Commissioners refused Boone's claim on the grounds that "he had failed to produce sufficient evidence that he had killed the highwayman James Towle."[9] There is speculation that the "K. F. Towle" who sat on the jury of Jack McCall was road agent Frank Towle. This seems to indicate that they were not the same individuals. The road agent's name was apparently James F. Towle.

The skull of Frank Towle was taken to the outskirts of Cheyenne and buried. A sunny, Sunday May afternoon brought a Mr. Clark out for a walk in the vicinity Towle's "grinning features" had been buried. Mr. Clark was startled to look up and see "the skull of that road agent dancing along and bobbing up and down among the cactus bushes." His hair reportedly stood on end, but he didn't budge an inch. Statue like, Mr. Clark remained in his position as the skull danced nearer and nearer to him. It was within his reach before he retreated some twenty feet. The skull continued its "dance of death," and Mr. Clark continued to watch. When the skull reached a small town of prairie dogs it suddenly stopped and the mystery unraveled. A huge prairie dog emerged from the skull and was soon joined by "fifteen or twenty lively little companions." All were soon engrossed in rolling and tumbling the skull around on the ground and Mr. Clark returned to Cheyenne. It was the final chapter of the story.[10]

1.   **Cheyenne Daily Leader,** September 14, 1878; **Black Hills Daily Times,** September 23, 1878, and September 14, 1878.
2.   Richard B. Hughes (Agnes Wright Spring, ed.), **Pioneer Years in the Black Hills,** p. 250.
3.   **Cheyenne Daily Leader,** op. cit.; **Black Hills Daily Times,** op. cit.
4.   It was returned when they learned Mr. Goldsworthy was a "working man."
5.   **Black Hills Daily Times,** September 14, 1878.
6.   **Cheyenne Daily Leader,** December 28, 1878; Agnes Wright Spring, **The Cheyenne-Black Hills State and Express Routes,** pp. 286-288. Nellie Snyder Yost, ed., **Boss Cowman,** p. 305, identifies Frank James, as did Boone May. Lemmon, however, stated Boone's companion was Billie Samples (sic).
7.   **Cheyenne Daily Leader,** December 28, 1878; **Black Hills Daily Times,** March 11, 1879; Spring, op. cit.
8.   **Black Hills Daily Times,** August 18, 1880. **Wyoming,** American Guide Series, p. 223.
9.   **Black Hills Daily Times,** March 11, 1879.
10.   **Cheyenne Daily Leader,** May 21, 1879.

THE GEORGE AXELBY GANG AND "THE STONEVILLE BATTLE"

The 14th of February, 1884, found about eight inches of snow on the ground at Stoneville, Montana Territory. Stoneville had remained essentially unchanged from the way "Limestone" Wilson had found it four years earlier while hunting buffalo: "The place consisted of seven or eight rough log shacks, the largest one being owned by Lou Stone who ran a store and post office in one end of the building and a saloon in the other, the two being divided by a partition."[1]

The George Axelby Gang was "bellied up to the bar" this particular morning; not an unusual occurrence for the place Wilson characterized as "a sort of rendezvous for hunters, horse thieves, road agents and whiskey traders." Humphrey Hood, a former "Hashknife" range boss, provided the friendly face behind the bar as the temperature dropped to -25° outside. Axelby was accompanied by his lieutenant, William "Billy-the-Kid" McCarthy, "Bronco" or "Bad Land Charlie", Alex Grady, Hank Campbell, and Henry Tuttle.[2] Jesse Pruden was conspicuous by his absence.

With the exception of one gang member, name unknown, who was lynched near Custer, Dakota Territory, the gang had operated relatively unhampered.[3] So unhampered, in fact, that they began receiving press coverage in such far away places as New York City, where they captured the imagination of one **New York Sun** writer:

Mr. Axelby is said to be at the head of a trusty band as fearless and as lawless as himself. The Little Missouri and Powder River districts are the theater of his operations. An

Indian is Mr. Axelby's detestation. He kills him at sight if he can. He considers that Indians have no right to own ponies and he takes their ponies whenever he can. Mr. Axelby has repeatedly announced his determination not to be taken alive. The men of the frontier say he bears a charmed life, and the hairbreadth's 'scapes of which they have made him the hero, are numerous and of the wildest stamp.[4]

On Febuary 3, 1884, Jesse Pruden was arrested in Miles City, Montana Territory, by Custer County Sheriff J. W. Johnson. Pruden, arrested for the theft of Indian ponies from the Pine Ridge Indian Reservation, later said of his arrest and the subsequent fight at Stoneville:

> I was arrested and in custody ten or twelve days, pending the arrival of Deputy Marshal Jos. Ryan, on whose arrival we left Miles City February 14th, the day of the affray at the Little Missouri. Pending the arrival of Marshal Ryan, George Axelby heard of my arrest, that I was being taken to Deadwood much against my will, and resolved to rescue me at some point on the road. I was apprised of this intention by a friend, the night before leaving Miles for Deadwood. Before leaving Miles, I told Marshal Ryan that I would be rescued. This bit of information seemed to amuse the marshal very much, and he said it was just what he wanted; that, in that event, he would bag the whole 'caboodle' . . .[5]

Pruden was not the only one who had been apprised of the Axelby Gang's intention to free him. Someone at Stoneville had warned Sheriff Johnson that "something was in the wind." Johnson sent two of his deputies to accompany Ryan until he was met by Dakota authorities sent from Spearfish or Deadwood. He had previously wired the Marshal's Office at Deadwood that an attempt to free Pruden would be launched by "the lawless characters on Powder River and vicinity." Johnson's terse warning was relayed to Deputy U.S. Marshal Fred Willard at Spearfish. Upon receipt of the warning, a posse which consisted of Willard, Lawrence County Deputy Sheriff Jack O'Hara, and M. C. Alderbeau left immediately.[6]

A posse from Deadwood, headed by Deputy U.S. Marshal A. M. "Cap" Willard, Fred's brother, was also organized. The Deadwood posse, unable to reach Spearfish before that posse left, hurried on to overtake them. Unsuccessful in their attempt to overtake them on the road, the two posses unknowingly spent the night of the 13th at road ranches two miles apart.[7]

A. M. "Cap" Willard (left), and Fred Willard (right). (*Photo: Courtesy Wyoming State Archives, Museums, and Historical Dept.*)

O'Hara and Willard had left Alderbeau behind during the first leg of the long grueling ride. The men and horses were put to the ultimate test; snow covered the ground, the gullies were drifted full and it was below zero with a stock killing wind blowing.

Fred Willard and O'Hara immediately went to Stone's house when they arrived in Stoneville. They were told that the gang was still in the saloon, some two hundred yards from Stone's house. The outlaws soon emerged from the saloon and "leading one horse packed and one saddled, supposed for Pruden to ride, started up the road.'' Aware that this would probably be their best opportunity to stop the gang, but unaware that reinforcements were nearby, O'Hara and Fred Willard ran out of Stone's house and fired at all the outlaws they could see. The surprised outlaws were quick to return their fire.**8**

"Cap" Willard and Alderbeau were near enough to hear the first shots. Willard dug his spurs into his exhausted horse and dashed ahead to, according to the **Black Hills Times,** give the gang "a lesson in morality, civilization, and republican institutions.'' One of his first shots was effective. "Tuttle . . . was mounted on a mule, and when the firing commenced, Mr. Mule began to buck, and turn around and

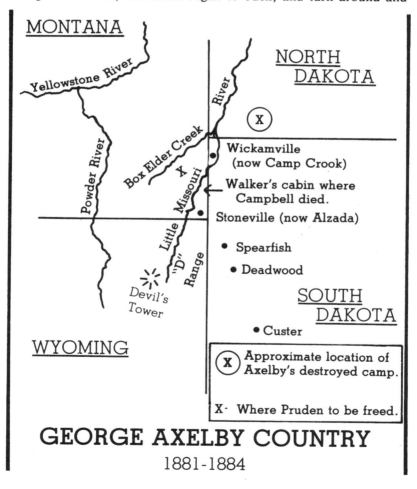

GEORGE AXELBY COUNTRY
1881-1884

around, in a circle. During this circus performance Tuttle was shot in the left elbow, breaking his arm badly. He fell off the mule and crawled to Shuster's house . . . where a cowboy bandaged his arm so tightly that inflammation set in, and (he) was glad to surrender in the morning."[9]

One of the lawmen, perhaps the most popular of the three, died. "Billy-the-Kid" was slow in getting saddled up that morning. He was about to leave the corral when the shooting matinee started, and bystanders saw him duck behind a large corral post. From his vantage point he had the lawmen caught in a cross fire, and was the only member of the gang to be able to shoot effectively. One of his first shots struck Jack O'Hara. O'Hara, standing by Fred Willard, had

fired eight or nine shots before he was hit. He turned and said, "Fred, I staid with you as long as I could; give them the best you have." Ten minutes later, Mrs. Jack O'Hara was a widow. Another of "Billy-the-Kid's" shots passed through Fred Willard's coat, vest, and undershirt, but miraculously stopped before it broke the skin. Yet another passed so close to "Cap" Willard's ear that it made it sting.[10]

A. M. "Cap" Willard. *(Photo: Courtesy South Dakota State Historical Society.)*

A heavy snow was falling at the time and the gang disappeared into the brush, firing random potshots as they retreated. After the lawmen were out of range, the gang began shooting into a group of cowboys that had been standing in front of the store, but who had taken no part in the fight. The outlaws "killed one cowboy and wounded another so that they got him . . ."[11] The dead cowboy, William Cunningham, and the wounded one, Jack Harris, were both "D" hands. It was known that Axelby held a grudge against Cunningham and Axelby had threatened to kill him for his particularly conscientious effort to keep the Axelby Gang off "D" ranges. No motive was known for the shooting of Harris, who was shot through the thigh and lingered until the following August.[12]

A courier was dispatched to Spearfish to summon medical aid and reinforcements. Deputy U.S. Marshals Al Raymond and George Bartlett, accompanied by Drs. Babcock and Louthan with others left immediately after the call came in. The relief party arrived at Stoneville at three o'clock the morning of the 16th.[13] Unsure of the final outcome of the fight, they surrounded Stone's house. After they called for those inside to show themselves, Fred Willard appeared in the doorway. After a brief consultation it was decided that tracking could best be accomplished in the morning after their horses had rested. The body of Jack O'Hara lay in the next building. Cunningham had been buried the previous day. Drs. Babcock and Louthan attended to the wounds of Jack Harris and Henry Tuttle.

Tombstone of Jack O'Hara, Rose Hill Cemetery, Spearfish, popular deputy sheriff killed during Stoneville Battle. (*Photo: Author's.*)

Rubbing from O'Hara Tombstone.

The known wounds and subsequent movements of the outlaws were recounted for the benefit of the recent arrivals. Hank Campbell had sustained a serious head wound and fell, but rallied and crawled into the brush. George Axelby had been shot in the thigh; his horse shot from under him. Tuttle's arm was examined by the doctors, and was a serious wound. If any other members of the gang had been wounded it had gone unnoticed; however, it was certain that "Billy-the-Kid" had escaped unscathed.[14]

Former cowboy and buffalo hunter turned horsethief, George Axelby. (*Photo: Author's collection.*)

The next day it was learned that Axelby, with two or three others, had gone to Sheldon's cabin near Stoneville the night of the fight and obtained bandages, a coat and hat, and $40. Campbell had crawled down the iced over Little Missouri River five miles to the cabin of the James Walker family. There his wounds were treated to the best of Walker's abilities with no questions asked. From the Walker ranch, Campbell sent an urgent message to Humphrey Hood:

Dear Hood: I was badly wounded in the head during the fight yesterday and my horse killed. The boys were all shot to pieces and scattered. For God's sake, send me a horse by bearer as soon as it is dark enough to get away from the officers.[15]

"Cap" Willard obtained possession of the note and instructed Billy Chase, the bearer of the note, to deliver a horse to Campbell as he requested. A well armed posse followed Chase and the Trojan horse. As Chase entered Walker's cabin, the posse secreted themselves nearby. When Campbell emerged and prepared to mount the horse, a voice sang out, "Throw up your hands." Campbell turned and fired once in the direction of the voice before he fell, mortally wounded.

Although his body lay where it fell for two days, someone took the time to count his wounds. Fifteen.[16]

Frozen stiff, Campbell's body was brought into Stoneville on the third day, serving as a buckboard seat for two of the posse members. Upon their arrival in Stoneville they deposited their "seat" in front of the hotel, where it remained until the proprietress insisted that he be given a decent burial. Campbell was buried near the Little Missouri River at Stoneville. A bullet riddled board, to signify his violent death, served as a tombstone.[17]

It was first thought that Tuttle would "never be called upon to plead in the United States court," but under the care of Drs. Louthan and Babcock he lived and was taken to the hospital in Spearfish. On the night of February 26, the hospital was invaded by six to eight masked men who wore buffalo overcoats. They determined where Tuttle was sleeping, and after warning the other patients not to go outside until morning, removed Tuttle. In the first light of early morning the body of Henry Tuttle could be seen suspended from a tree overlooking Spearfish. Of the lynching one Spearfish citizen wrote, "The least criminal of the men who stood on that cliff of rocks . . . was the man that hanged."[18]

A posse met Ryan and his prisoner to escort them to Deadwood. Pruden was tried, with George Axelby in absentia, during the September term of U.S. District Court. Although four Indian witnesses identified Pruden as one of the men who had stolen their horses, the jury found Jesse Pruden not guilty. No verdict was returned in the case of George Axelby.[19]

The Axelby Gang remained quiet for one season, then "a half breed appeared at Sturgis, dusty, footsore, and mad clear through." He had located and cut out eight horses that had been stolen from him over a year earlier. Before he could get them back to his home range he was overtaken by a party of well-armed men. The men, whom he reported to be the Axelby Gang, "without ado, again set him on foot." It was the last anyone in the area heard of Axelby or "Billy-the-Kid" until 1889, although reports frequently were circulated that various lawmen had killed them shortly after the Stoneville Battle.[20]

The last man known to have seen Axelby and "Billy-the-Kid" was Texas-New Mexico rustler Martin M'Rose. M'Rose, a Texas born Pole, was no stranger to the "wide loop" himself. During the dozen or so years he was known as a rustler in northwestern Texas he was "credited" with the theft of 15,000 to 20,000 head of stock.[21] As related by A. P. "Ott" Black in **The End of the Long Horn Trail:**

I worked with Martin Marose (sic) in 1889 and he told me that Axelby and 'the Kid' rode into Clayton Wells, New Mexico, a short time afterward. They were bound for the Mexican border . . . Marose said they rode in and spread eight thousand dollars in greenbacks all over the inside of the house and made that adobe shack as hot as a furnace. As soon as the money dried they rode off to the south.[22]

If M'Rose knew more about Axelby and "the Kid" than he related to Black, it was a secret that he took to the grave with him. M'Rose was killed June 29, 1895, on the outskirts of El Paso, Texas, by lawmen Jeff Milton, Frank McMahan, and George Scarbourgh.[23]

"Bronco Charlie" returned to his dubious livelihood and became a statistic. He was one of sixty-one men shot and hung during a clean-up of rustlers in southeastern Montana and southwestern North Dakota. Five years after the "clean-up" the **Billings Gazette** recalled "Bronco Charlie's" demise: "Turkey Williams and Bronco Charlie were found hanging in the cottonwoods about ten miles above Miles City."[24]

1. William E. "Limestone" Wilson, "Blizzards and Buffalo — 1880", **Montana; The Magazine of Western History,** Vol. XIX, No. 1, January 1969, p. 38. Quoted with permission of Montana Historical Society.
2. Ibid.; Gang members identified by Jesse Pruden were Axelby, Tuttle, "Billy-the-Kid", and "Bad Land Charlie", **Yellowstone Journal,** March 1, 1884. Various other contemporary newspaper accounts add the names of Campbell and Grady.
3. Robert J. Casey, **The Black Hills and Their Incredible Characters,** p. 189; **Yellowstone Journal,** February 9, 1884.
4. **New York Sun** article quoted in Hagedorn's **Roosevelt in the Bad Lands,** p. 141. Although Hagedorn dated the article 1884, it probably appeared in 1883 when Axelby was at the height or his career.
5. **Yellowstone Journal,** March 1, 1884.
6. **Black Hills Times,** February 16, 1884; **Yellowstone Journal,** February 23, 1884.
7. **Black Hills Times,** February 16, 1884; John O. Bye, **Back Trailing in the Heart of the Short-Grass Country,** p. 64. **Back Trailing** contains four pieces by four different writers about the Stoneville Battle. This author has used it as a reference only when the information could be verified by contemporary newspaper accounts.
8. **Black Hills Times,** February 20, 1884.
9. Ibid.
10. Ibid.; **Black Hills Times,** February 16, 1884; **Belle Fourche Times,** February 14, 1918; **Black Hills Times,** February 19, 1884.
11. **Yellowstone Journal,** March 1, 1884. This account, given to the **Yellowstone Journal** by the two deputies who escorted Joe Ryan, is one

of the most reliable contemporary accounts. **Black Hills Times,** February, 19, 20, 1884.

12. **Black Hills Times,** February 19, 20, 1884.
13. **Black Hills Times,** February 20, 1884. An account of "The Stoneville Battle" appeared in **Literary Digest,** March 11, 1911. The article was attributed to George Bartlett, who since had assumed the title "Captain." Although all contemporary accounts, as does Brown and Willard's **Black Hills Trails,** indicate that Bartlett did not arrive until well after the last shot had been fired, he claimed: To have led the posse; that Axelby died one-half an hour after he was wounded; that he, Bartlett, and he alone killed Campbell; that he was wounded, and nursed back to health by none other than Calamity Jane, etc.

   Although "Cap" Willard was indignant, and rightfully so, about Bartlett's article (see: **Black Hills Trails,** pp. 305-306 and 312), he wasn't above overstating his own importance. Willard states on p. 312, ". . . at Fort Meade a troop of the Seventh United States Cavalry was ordered out, **but my coming in stopped the expedition."** Troops were called out, according to the **Sturgis Weekly Record,** February 22, 1884, but the 1878 "posse comitatus law" prevented any military intervention in civilian matters and, therefore, no troops were sent to Stoneville.

14. **Black Hills Times,** February 20, 1884.
15. Ibid.; **Yellowstone Journal,** March 20, 1884; Annie Tallent, **The Black Hills; or The Last Hunting Grounds of the Dakotahs,** p. 423. Tallent calls Stoneville, Montana Territory, Stonewall, Montana.
16. **Yellowstone Journal,** February 23, 1884; **Black Hills Times,** February 20, 1884; Bye, op. cit., p. 63.
17. Ibid.
18. **Black Hills Times,** February 20, 28, 29, 1884.
19. **Black Hills Times,** April 22, September 14, 1884.
20. **Black Hills Times,** June 19, 1884. Bartlett, op. cit., states Axelby was killed at Stoneville and Fred Willard killed "Billy-the-Kid" a month later. **Black Hills Trails** state both were killed about four months later by Fred Willard. No contemporary accounts indicate that either is true, and their deaths would not have gone unreported; nor would the Willards or Bartlett killed them, and let it go unreported.
21. James W. Freeman, ed., **Prose and Poetry of the Live Stock Industry,** p. 631.
22. Black, op. cit. It should be noted Clayton Wells was never anything more than a cattle watering hole.
23. Leon C. Metz, "Hardin Called West's Most Dangerous Gunman", **El Paso Times,** August 20, 1972.
24. "The Montana Stranglers", **True Western Adventures,** August 1967, p. 31, quotes the undated **Billings Gazette** article. Wallis Huidekoper, **The Land of the Dacotahs,** p. 15, puts the number at sixty-one. As the son of HT Ranch owner A. C. Huidekoper, he was in a position to know.

ROBERT "REDDY" McKIMIE

Red haired Robert "Reddy" McKimie, also known as "Little Reddy, From Texas," was an experienced road agent when he arrived in the Black Hills. Seth Bullock claimed that McKimie had deserted the army, then

> joined a gang who were depredating along the stage route in Utah, murdering and robbing whenever opportunity offered. He was finally captured and sentenced to fifteen years imprisonment in the Utah Penitentiary for killing a man in southern Utah. He made his escape in company with Jack Williamson, another convict . . . He (McKimie) escaped after he served nearly a year.

McKimie admitted that he had escaped, but denied that he killed a guard in the process. McKimie said that he had put a dummy in his bed, then hid in the prison well until it was safe. He said that Williamson had struck the guard over the head with an iron bar, and "got away" immediately afterward.[1]

After his escape McKimie lived in Denver for a time where he was "regarded as a peaceable, law-abiding citizen." In 1875 he was employed as a utility man by B. L. Ford at the Inter Ocean Hotel in Cheyenne. Although McKimie "was a general favorite," Ford fired McKimie when he could not tolerate his impudence any longer. McKimie went to the Black Hills from Cheyenne, and upon a visit with Ford said that he was "doing well in the Hills and expected to 'get rich sometime'."[2]

McKimie's red hair and his eagerness to participate in any scheme, no matter how reckless, earned him the nickname "Little

Reddy, from Texas'' although he was from Ohio. McKimie once rode
a horse stolen in Wyoming into Deadwood where he offered it for sale
at such a ridiculously low price Sheriff Seth Bullock's suspicions were
aroused. Upon investigation, Bullock learned the horse was stolen and
jailed McKimie. Since the value of the horse, which was returned to its
rightful owner, was less than the cost of prosecution, McKimie was

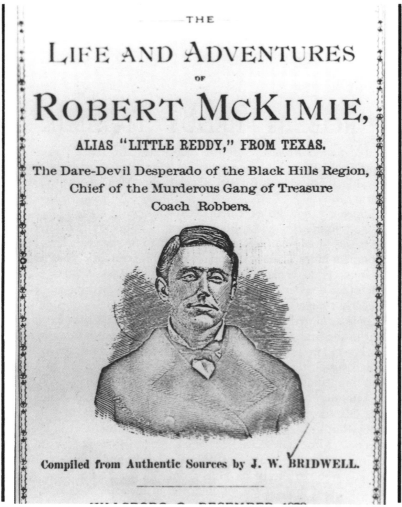

Frontspiece of The Life and Adventures of Robert McKimie. A second book, written
by the man who "gave them away," was published the following month. (*Photo:
Author's collection.*)

freed. McKimie said later that Seth Bullock was the only man he was ever afraid of.[3]

"Reddy" loafed about Deadwood, plotting, scheming, and gambling. On at least one occasion, "Reddy" walked away from the gambling tables a big winner: " 'Reddy' was in luck yesterday, drawing out about $500 from two games, striking eight double cards for $25 each in one deal." In Deadwood McKimie became acquainted with members of the Joel Collins-Sam Bass Gang. Their robberies in the Black Hills before McKimie joined them are a footnote to history. Charles L. Martin's **A Sketch of Sam Bass** put the figure, probably quite realistically, at "about $100." McKimie joined the gang in February, 1877, and was ostracized by them in late March for the act he is most remembered for in Black Hills history.[4]

On March 25, 1877, five members of the gang, Collins, Bass, McKimie, Frank Towle and Jim Berry or Bill Heffridge, planned to hold-up the "up" coach (Deadwood bound) near Deadwood. The coach, with popular young Johnny Slaughter at the reins, had experienced trouble out of Hill City and was far behind schedule. As the coach came down Whitewood Canyon, near the present day Pluma, five masked men walking in the road suddenly wheeled and ordered Slaughter to "Halt." Slaughter attempted to "wheel up." One of the robbers, "Reddy", stood near the "leaders," the first pair of horses in a six-horse span. The "leaders" became nervous and "Reddy" pulled the trigger of his shotgun. Slaughter tumbled from the boot, mortally wounded. Walter Iler, a passenger riding "on the boot" with Slaughter, was also hit by the buckshot, but was not seriously wounded. The team ran away at the shot and became so badly tangled in their harnesses that they stopped before the coach tipped. Iler and other passengers untangled the harnesses and Iler guided the stage into Deadwood. It was after midnight when they arrived, but even at that late hour a posse was quickly organized to look for Slaughter and the gang. The body of Johnny Slaughter was found where it fell, but no trace of the gang was found. Twelve of thirteen buckshot were said to have formed a perfect circle above Slaughter's heart.[5]

A funeral was held in Deadwood's Grand Central Hotel April 4, with Reverend Norcross officiating. A second funeral, held in Cheyenne April 4, was reported to have been the largest in Cheyenne's history. Luke Voorhees provided six matched white horses for the hearse. Slaughter, a son of City Marshal and Mrs. John Slaughter, had been one of the most popular drivers on the line. At the young age of twenty-seven he had been assigned to one of the most hazardous

portions of the route because of
his ability. Slaughter was buried
in the Lakeview Cemetery in
Cheyenne. On May 1 the **Cheyenne Daily Leader** reported the
sudden death of his grief stricken
mother. She was laid to rest next
to her son.[6]

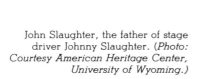

John Slaughter, the father of stage
driver Johnny Slaughter. (*Photo:
Courtesy American Heritage Center,
University of Wyoming.*)

McKimie's sudden and ill-advised shooting turned the gang
against him. They had a $500 reward — ''dead or alive'' — on them.
It was also learned that one of the passengers was carrying $15,000 to
Stebbin, Wood & Company's Deadwood branch. After a lengthy
debate whether or not to kill McKimie, they agreed to let him live, but
ordered him out of the gang and the Black Hills.[7]

McKimie next joined forces with Dunc Blackburn and Clark Pelton who were robbing stages with varied success near Hat Creek.
After McKimie left them near the Point of Rocks station (see Blackburn and Pelton chapter) he and a disreputable woman went to St.

Point of Rocks station, Wyoming. (*Photo: Courtesy Wyoming State Archives,
Museums, and Historical Department.*)

Louis. McKimie said that he gave her $1,000 in St. Louis and they parted. After a brief sojourn into Texas, McKimie traveled to Phila-delphia and either exchanged the dust or had it minted. He then returned to his old Ohio haunts where he claimed to have become rich in the cattle business. In quick succession McKimie married Clara Ferguson, bought a farm, then traded the farm for a store.[8]

Oddly, the arrest of McKimie was related to the Joel Collins-Sam Bass Gang's $60,000 Big Spring, Nebraska, train robbery. The date of his return, not long after the September 18th robbery, and his free-wheeling business transactions aroused the suspicions of a neighbor. The neighbor, who knew of the robbery, contacted Ogalala, Nebras-ka, store clerk cum detective, M. F. Leach. Leach traveled to Hills-boro where his investigation cleared McKimie of the train robbery, but convinced him that McKimie was a Black Hills road agent. Leach advised Luke Voorhees and Seth Bullock, operating the Black Hills Detective Agency since his defeat by Johnny Manning in the election, of McKimie's whereabouts. Bullock traveled to Hillsboro and Leach continued his pursuit of train robbers Joel Collins, Sam Bass, Jim Berry, Jack Davis, Bill Heffridge and Tom Nixon.[9]

In Hillsboro, Bullock was introduced to McKimie as "Mr. Some-body, who was dealing in his line of goods," by deputy U.S. Marshal Lyle. Convinced that McKimie was his man, Bullock arrested him. Bullock and Lyle lodged McKimie in jail which proved to be a grave tactical error. Bullock should have either immediately put McKimie on a train bound for Wyoming or obtained a requisition from the governor of Ohio before McKimie's arrest. (For a detailed account of the legal ramifications of McKimie's premature jailing see: **Life and Adventures of Robert McKimie**, pp. 10-11.) Mired in legal difficulties, Bullock wired for Luke Voorhees' assistance. Voorhees traveled to Ohio, but the case was bound for the Ohio Supreme Court and there was little he could do. He left Bullock in Ohio to protect Wyoming's interests and returned to Cheyenne.[10]

The Ohio authorities were referred to as "the Buckeye bobbies" in the Cheyenne press, partially because they refused to believe that McKimie was a dangerous man. The **Black Hills Daily Times** also got into the act, later using Seth's "interesting" description of the Ohioians: "They think Christ was a Democrat, and frequently asked him who He ran against for the Presidency."[11]

McKimie's friends and wife were allowed to visit him whenever they wished. Clara McKimie roamed in and out of his cell until a revolver and cartridges were found in a search of the cell while they were at a court appearance. No longer allowed such freedom, she remained in his cell with him. It was not thought, however, that she had provided him with them. The conditions were perfect for McKimie's February 11th escape. His wife was visiting the jailer's family. Seth Bullock was out of town visiting friends. Sheriff Newell was also out of town. When Mr. Newell, the sheriff's father, and a porter entered the cell to fill the coal box, McKimie sprang at them with a revolver. He later said his escape was "as easy as falling off a log." Mr. Newell had fired a shot at McKimie when he reached the gate, and McKimie's bloodied cigar case was found nearby the next morning. When Sheriff Newell and Bullock arrived in Hillsboro they offered rewards totaling $600 for McKimie's recapture.[12]

McKimie's friends hid him out and assisted him in disguising himself. Black dye was applied to his red hair and a "bunch of hair from his whiskers under his chin" was fashioned into a mustache. The dye was applied so liberally that it caused his skin to splotch. It was over a week before he could venture out. After the splotches disappeared, McKimie encountered Bullock, Sheriff Newell, and deputy U.S. Marshal Lyle, but his identity was not detected.[13]

McKimie left the Hillsboro area and was joined in Richmond, Virginia, by his wife. They traveled throughout the South and to the Bermuda Islands. They ran out of money in the Bermudas and McKimie spent forty-one days in a debtor's prison before the American Counsel arranged for his "working passage" to New York aboard a steamer. He returned to Ohio where he and a companion robbed an eighty-year-old man of $90. McKimie returned to the Bermuda Islands for his wife. She remained on the East Coast after their return, while McKimie again went to Ohio. In Ohio he and his gang engaged in a lengthy, very active robbery and burglary spree that encompassed several counties.[14]

Sheriff Newell. (*From:* **The Life and Adventures of Robert McKimie.**)

McKimie was arrested in late November after smoke was seen emitting from a supposedly empty cabin near Hillsboro. One hundred to one hundred fifty men surrounded the cabin, and McKimie was captured after a brief fight. McKimie, using the only man who was courageous enough to enter the cabin as a shield, was shot in the chest. McKimie was shot several more times before he finally surrendered.

Chained, with his arms and legs pinioned with rope, McKimie was taken to jail. McKimie was protected from a lynch mob by Sheriff Newell, and proudly displayed his wounds; even his old ones. He held up his right hand to Mr. Newell and told him, "This is some of your work."[15]

Cabin where McKimie was captured. (*From:* **The Life and Adventures of Robert McKimie.**)

When the governor of Ohio revoked Wyoming's requisition for McKimie, the counties where his recent crimes had been committed began vying for the right to try him. Bullock, who had returned to Deadwood when it became apparent McKimie would not be recaptured immediately, returned to Ohio and visited McKimie in his cell. Although it had been reported that McKimie's greatest fear was "that he will be taken back to the Black Hills," Bullock found the opposite to be true.

"How would you like to go to Cheyenne with me, Bob?" Bullock asked.

"Oh, first rate. I am in a pretty tight place here, and they are going to give me a 'lifer' if they can," McKimie replied. It was a rhetorical question and reply. Bullock already knew that Ohio would not give McKimie up.

The entire conversation was not that cordial. McKimie warned Bullock that, "I am going to 'crease' you if I ever get the chance."

"All right," Bullock replied. "If you ever get the chance I expect you to; but you know damned well that I ain't afraid of you."

"That's so," McKimie agreed, "but if ever we come together on anything like equal chances, one or the other has got to die."[16]

They never came together on anything like equal chances. McKimie was tried and found guilty of an assortment of crimes in

JAMES "FLY-SPECK BILLY" FOWLER

Veterans of Montana's Alder Gulch were grumbling as early as 1875 that before a "regular mining camp" could be established on French Creek, "the pine tree will need a blossom or two."[1]

Tom Milligan narrowly averted becoming the first blossom in March, 1876, when he killed his partner, Alex Shaw. Milligan and Shaw were passing the time by pulling on a whiskey bottle and shooting at an old bucket. The whiskey eventually had an effect on Milligan's aim, and Shaw fell. The surviving one escaped a lynch mob when he announced that he was a Free Mason and reminded his fraternal brothers that they were bound to protect him. Milligan was fined twenty-five dollars, all the money he had, for discharging a fire-

Custer, c. 1885. *(Photo: Courtesy South Dakota State Historical Society.)*

arm within the city limits, and warned out of town. Thus, Custer City recorded its first killing, but the pine tree remained undecorated.[2]

Ellis T. "Doc" Peirce recalled that it was also in 1876 when he nursed a friendless young man, delirious with mountain fever, back to health at the free hospital he was operating in Custer City. His patient's recovery was slow and took several weeks. He told Peirce that his name was Fowler and "intimated that I had not selected the best material to bestow my charity upon," but "seemed to feel grateful." As a token of his esteem he presented Peirce with an order for his horse, saddle, and bridle, which were held for him at the livery, pending his recovery. Before Peirce could claim the outfit it was stolen by an unknown thief. Fowler was "very indignant" about the theft, and left Peirce vowing to "bring back a lock of hair of the fellow who stole" it. Peirce soon heard that Fowler was near Fort Reno where he avenged the theft of his outfit by stealing nine horses from the innocent party of D. K. Snively.[3]

Ellis Taylor Peirce. Of him Annie D. Tallent wrote, "With an acute sense of the ridiculous there was no occurrence so pathetic that 'Doc' could not detect, without the aid of a Roentgen ray, a thread of comic running through its warp and woof." *(Photo: Courtesy South Dakota State Historical Society.)*

One of Fowler's last lawless acts was the robbing and beating of an old woman at Sturgis, where he had been known by the name Majors. It was his drunken method of repaying her for befriending him in much the same way Peirce had.[4]

After beating and robbing the old woman, little time elapsed before Fowler met Abe Barnes, a freighter on his way to Custer City. **The Custer Chronicle** reporter who wrote of the events that linked the pair together penned a masterpiece of early Black Hills journalism.

The following is a verbatim account, as it appeared in the **Chronicle,** February 12, 1881:

Last Sunday night was the occasion of the most thrilling and exciting scene that Custer has witnessed since her resurrection. A cold blooded and unprovoked murder was committed followed almost immediately by the lynching of the murderer. The facts of the case will be made more intelligible to the reader by commencing the account with the first appearance of Fowler, alias 'Fly Specked Billy,' in the company of his victim:

Abe Barnes, freighter residing at Kearney Junction, Nebraska, and engaged in the business of hauling freight, was coming towards Custer. When about 20 miles below here he was joined, on the road, by a man known to many of our old residents, as 'Fly Specked Billy,' a desperate character, an outlaw, and formerly connected with Lame Johnny, of infamous notoriety. Billy informed the train that he had just left a freight outfit, going from Deadwood to Sidney, and that he desired to visit Custer. He was allowed to mess with the train, partly through fear and partly for the sake of old acquaintanceship. They arrived in town Sunday forenoon, and Billy at once made inquiries as to who were the peace officers, the sheriff, etc. Having fully posted himself on this point, and keeping an eye upon their motions as he feared arrest for some of his former crimes, he began going about from one saloon to another, making himself generally disagreeable by his abusive language and threatening movements.

A game of Spanish monte soon attracted him and a bluff for a fight was soon made. The bystanders prevented blows being struck at this time, although only one or two were acquainted with the dangerous character of the man. Billy then went to Barnes and asked him to let him have his pistol, claiming that he needed it to protect himself from some threatened violence. Barnes rather reluctantly gave it to him, thus unwittingly furnishing him the weapon to take his, Barnes', life. After procuring the revolver, a large Colt's forty-five, he went on a hunt for a victim, and from his actions seemed not to care who it might be. He had apparently got himself to a point of vindictiveness that could only be allayed by taking someone's life. It had probably been some time since he had killed anyone, and he was afraid he might get his hand out. About every man who saw him during the evening had the pistol stuck into his breast and was obliged to obey his caprice. Finally about 10 o'clock in going into Geo. Palmer's saloon he encountered some stranger whom he ordered to come in and take a drink, at the same time laying the revolver over the man's shoulder and firing three shots into the building opposite. Palmer, it seems, had ordered him out of the place an hour or two previous, and seeing him now enter with a pistol in hand, the other man also having a pistol out, thought it a concerted plan to suit themselves, but having no pistol was unable to do anything. Billy amused himself for some time by cocking a letting down the hammer, while the muzzle was within a foot or two of Palmer's breast, at the same time keeping a sharp watch in the large mirror to see that no one approached him from behind. Happening to notice a slight movement on the part of William Summers, who was sitting down near him, he seized him by the collar and sticking the pistol against his breast he pulled the trigger. Fortunately the hammer came down on one of the exploded cartridges and Summers was not the victim. He then turned towards Mr. Eby asking him if he wanted some of it. Eby didn't particularly hanker after any, he said. Billy then walked over to where Mr. Barnes was playing billiards and caught him by the collar, at the same time holding the pistol against his right breast. The words, "Come and take a drink," and the shot were simultaneous. Barnes cried out, "Oh, I am shot," ran a few steps and fell, expiring in about fifteen minutes. After his first ejaculation he never spoke. Billy made a run for the door intending to escape. Mr. Eby, however, grappled with him as he passed, and Red Moor struck a furious blow at the wretch's head with a Colt's pistol. The first blow fell on Eby's hand, nearly crushing it. The second was delivered with better effect, just as the door was reached, and he fell into the arms of John T. Code, the sheriff, who was just rushing in, having heard the shot. The prisoner was then taken down to Pat McHugh's place and bound. The news spread rapidly, and the people seemed to be in a state of more than ordinary indignation.

Code feared an attempt to lynch his man, and accordingly kept him at Pat McHugh's until the crowd has (sic) dispersed. The lights were then put out, and he waited about an hour after that before he attempted to remove his prisoner to his cabin, the jail being in no condition to put a prisoner in. He then started out the back door, having with him as deputies Frank Peters, Wm. Quinn and Pat McHugh. They had their prisoner bound tightly, and were consequently obliged to carry him. Arriving at the door of Code's cabin they were entering with as much haste as possible, when the avengers sprang out from every possible place of conceal-ment, and before Code could say a word, some half dozen disguised men were sitting down on him and as many more on his assistants, while the prisoner was spinning towards the nearest tree as rapidly as twenty men could haul him. Code and his men were thrust into the cabin, and what then occur-red can only be gleaned by the after discoveries.

Code soon came up Main Street and procured the assis-tance of the coroner and one or two others. They followed the tracks over to the edge of the timer (sic) across French Creek, where they found 'Fly Specked Billy' dangling from a pine tree, and no evidence of any living human being around. Judge Lynch had executed his inexorable sentence cleverly and secretly. 'Fly Specked Billy," with his hands warm with the blood of his unoffending victim, had paid the penalty, and his soul, if such as he have souls, and fled to the tortures of an eternity of punishment. The body was cut down and brought into town. No noise was heard, and but few were awakened, while any portion of the double tragedy was being enacted.[5]

One of the three shots "Fly Specked Billy" indiscriminately fired from Palmer's Saloon buried itself in a door-post John Young Nelson had been leaning against only moments earlier. Nelson claimed to have been a member of the lynch mob, but erred when he stated that "Fly Specked Billy" was taken from the saloon and lynched in "a sort of instantaneous court-martial."[6]

Nelson and Peirce both vividly recalled "Fly Specked Billy's" passiveness once he was in the hands of the lynch minded mob. "I think Billy himself was the calmest and most collected of the lot," Nelson wrote. "He made no resistance after we first grabbed him, and was still puffing at his cigar as we led him along. He watched the preparations without moving a muscle, and it was only as he was hoisted into mid-air that his cigar fell from his lips."[7]

DEATH'S ROUND-UP,

BY REVOLVER AND ROPE

A Law Abiding Citizen Shot by a Horse-thief.

The Sheriff and Deputies Over-powered, Their Prisoner Taken, and

A Murderer and Judge Lynch Become Acquainted.

"Fly Specked Billy" Transformed into a Pine Cone, with the Blood of Abe Barnes still warm on his hands.

Twenty Masked Men Send Him Over The Range.

Custer Chronicle, February 12, 1881

Peirce noted that the only resistance "Fly Specked Billy" made was "a desperate effort to kick his boots off." Earlier that day, full of brave maker, a gun most certainly in his hand, he had vowed he would never "die with his boots on."[8]

John Young Nelson toured the United States and Europe with Buffalo Bill's "Wild West Show." Nelson, seated left on stage, was the driver of "The Deadwood Stage" in the show. *(Photo: Courtesy Nebraska State Historical Society.)*

Although the coroner's jury ruled that "Fly Specked Billy" died from "strangulation at the hands of some person or persons unknown," one Custerite felt more — and a different explanation was called for. He wrote to a Deadwood friend that "Fly Specked Billy" had died of exposure; he had been "found the next morning hanging to a limb across French Creek, and the night being cold he froze to death."[9]

By February 19th the **Chronicle's** Black Hills exchanges comments were printed in a column entitled "What They Think of It." From the **Deadwood Press** came the comment that "the county has been saved several hundred dollars." And the **Times'** staff "thinks the hanging was all right, and as usual, express their willingness to take a drink at someone else's expense. None of that force will ever be shot for refusing a drink."[10]

On the home front, Custer was reported to have a ghost. The **Chronicle** reported: "We have it from good authority that the ghost of 'Fly Specked Billy' is to be seen walking in the neighborhood of the place where he was hung."[11] Fly Speck Billy's burial, near French Creek, was paid for by the county. Later the graves from the small cemetery along French Creek were moved to the present cemetery, but no grave is designated as being that of Custer's most "infamous desperado."[12]

Photo: Courtesy S.D. Division of Tourism.

1. **Helena** (Montana) **Weekly Herald,** September 2, 1875.
2. Ellis T. Peirce, "Odd Characters and Incidents in the Black Hills During the 70's," Peirce is the correct spelling, see Joseph C. Rosa's **They Called Him Wild Bill,** p. 299, which deals with the spelling in footnote 42.
3. Peirce, op. cit.
4. **Custer Chronicle,** February 19, 1881.
5. **Custer Chronicle,** February 12, 1881. An abbreviated version of this article appeared in Robert J. Casey's **The Black Hills and Their Incredible Characters,** p. 190-192. Unfortunately, the facsimile headline placed the murder-lynching as happening one month before it occurred. I seriously doubt that 'Fly Specked Billy' was a regular member of "Lame Johnny's" gang. "Lame Johnny" was a horse thief, but a professional one who would have had little use for an outlaw whose criminal tendencies came out with alcohol. Also, nothing in my research has indicated that "Fly Specked Billy" was a road agent, a category he has been placed in by some modern histories.
6. Harrington O'Reilly, **Fifty Years on the Trail,** pp. 275-276. As can be seen in the **Chronicle** account, he was taken from Pat McHugh's place. There was nothing "instantaneous" about it.
7. Nelson, op. cit.
8. Peirce, op. cit.
9. Letter, Charles Shankland to John Gaston, reprinted in **The Custer Chronicle ,** February 19, 1881; **Custer Chronicle,** February 12, 1881.
10. **Custer Chronicle,** February 19, 1881.
11. Ibid.
12. Ibid.; Mrs. Carl (Jessie) Sundstrom to author, June 24, 1980.

THE BELLE FOURCHE
BANK ROBBERY

The Butte County Bank, Belle Fourche, South Dakota, c. 1904.
(Photo: Author's Collection.)

On September 7, 1876 the Northfield, Minnesota bank caper went sour for the James-Younger gang. Bill Chadwell and Clell Miller were killed. Later Charlie Pitts was killed by the posse which left the Youngers; Bob, Jim and Cole, suffering from twenty collective wounds. Only Frank and Jesse James escaped unscathed.[1]

Grat and Bob Dalton, Bill Powers and Dick Broadwell died in Coffeyville, Kansas, October 5, 1892 after running into a dead end alley during their ill-fated attempt to rob two banks simultaneously. Emmett Dalton, the sole survivor, received a life sentence.[2]

When "the Curry gang" botched the June 27, 1897 robbery of the Butte County Bank the editor of the **Belle Fourche Times** was left to ponder a perplexing problem, one which he felt could have a national impact. "If 25 men, armed to the teeth, succeeded in killing a horse belonging to one of their own number, how many men will be required to whip Spain, in the event of war with that country?" he philosophically inquired.[3]

J. H. Chapman, C. A. Dana, Rev. Clough, E. M. Mitchell and Sam Arnold were in the bank waiting to transact business when the bank officially opened. As Cashier A. H. Marble and accountant Tinchnor were preparing for the day's business three or four men, their guns drawn, burst into the bank yelling, "Hold up your hands."[4]

Those inside readily complied with the order, but as Mr. Marble testified later, the gang seemed to be at a complete loss about what they should do next. "They seemed rattled, running from one man to another, telling them to hold up their hands; they did not seem to do much of anything except run from one man to another."[5]

Marble grabbed a revolver which was hidden near his elbow. He pointed it at the nearest intruder and squeezed the trigger. The minor explosion he expected was reduced to a lowly "click" as the bullet misfired.[6] Good authority had it that, his heroics failing, the only thing preventing Marble's arms from being any higher in the air was his height, or rather, his lack of it.[7]

Cashier Arthur Marble proved to be a real "heller with a gun" once he obtained some good ammunition. *(Photo: Courtesy Tri-State Museum, Belle Fourche, South Dakota.)*

Rev. Clough who was back of the cashier's screen writing a letter started forward at the unusual amount of noise. He was immediately confronted by a ''row of six-shooter muzzles'' and ordered to put up his hands also.

"Why, I'm only a poor Methodist preacher," he assured the gang. "You don't want anything of me."

"Preacher be damned," came the terse reply. "Put up your hands."

Discretion being the better part of valor, it was said later, the Reverend, when he discovered how lightly the gang regarded the cloth, ran into the bank vault.[8]

Alanson Giles, from his hardware store almost opposite the bank, saw the men's hands in the air over the window's half curtains. Realizing that something was wrong at the bank Giles ran across the street and opened the bank door. The interior of the bank bristled with six-shooters and Giles made a hasty retreat back to his store with one of the robbers in close pursuit.[9]

A Mr. Tracy, whose testimony would later identify Tom O'Day as a member of the gang, saw Giles and his pursuer and went to get a closer look-see. "I thought it was some kind of joke," he testified.[10]

Giles ran out the back door of his store and sounded the alarm that the bank was being robbed. At this Tom O'Day and Walter Punteney stepped out of the bank and began shooting up and down the street and into the stores of Giles' and the Gay Brothers. At the sound of the shooting, O'Day's horse, which had been left unhitched, ran off to join those of the fleeing robbers, leaving O'Day on foot.[11]

In their hasty departure one of the gang had the presence of mind to scoop up the precious little money the robbery netted: ninety-seven dollars.[12]

Although Mr. Marble's little pistol misfired in the bank, given some good ammunition, he proved to be a real heller with a gun. City Marshal Lee Brooks testified, "When I got there Mr. Marble was shooting, but the robbers were no where in sight."[13]

O'Day attempted to make the best of a bad situation and yelled at Brooks, "Don't shoot at the horses, they have one of mine." His ploy worked. No one realized O'Day was one of the bank robbers until he mounted an old mule and tried to urge it in the direction of Sundance Hill, the escape route taken by his companions. A small crowd gathered to witness the mule grudgingly begin to move, but emerge victorious — and go in the opposite direction.[14]

Tom O'Day displayed his "hang dog" look for the photographer. Photo from the Pinkerton Detective Agency, and used in their effort to land him. *(Photo: Author's Collection.)*

O'Day then abandoned the mule and set about to find a horse. He walked down the street and broke into a run at the vacant lot between Sebastian's Saloon and the **Times** office. Butcher Rusaw Bowman was the first to realize why O'Day's horse had joined the others and took up pursuit of him. He saw O'Day run past the "water closet", then turn around and duck into it. O'Day held his left hand in front of him, but Bowman was able to see a concealed revolver, half out of its holster. When O'Day emerged moments later, Bowman "threw down" on him and held him at bay until others arrived. Bowman then made a search of O'Day's pockets which yielded a pint of whiskey, some .44 calibre bullets and $392.50.[15]

From atop the elevator Frank Bennett observed a rider lagging behind the others. Bennett aimed his gun at the horse and squeezed the trigger.[16] Town blacksmith Joseph Miller had ridden barely two hundred yards in pursuit of the robbers before "sure-shot Bennett" killed his horse out from under him. Miller's problems were not over; it was with considerable difficulty that the angry townspeople were refrained from shooting Miller before he was recognized.[17]

Early Belle Fourche lumberman and City Councilman Frank Bennett. *(Photo: Courtesy Tri-State Museum, Belle Fourche, South Dakota.)*

O'Day's net loss: His freedom; his nickel-plated Colt .44 (with shells and holster, fished from the "water closet"); his horse (stolen); his gear (probably came with the horse); and the $392.50 found in his pockets. All no doubt flashed through his mind as he saw the rest of "the boys" ride out of sight over Sundance Hill.

O'Day's horse, shot in the foreleg, was found tied to a fence on Sundance Hill. Two quarts of whiskey, good whiskey according to Mr. Tracy, were found in the saddlebags.[18] And how did Mr. Tracy know that it was good whiskey? That came out at the hearing — in an unusual bit of testimony — when Mr. Tracy inadvertently admitted to being a connoisseur of bad whiskey:

Mr. Tracy: "I just happened to be looking at the whiskey he (O'Day) carried; that was how I came to notice him."
Defense Attorney: "That was good whiskey?"
Mr. Tracy: "Yes sir — I have not tried it."[19]

The posse, which numbered as high as 100 at times, had sight of the gang at frequent intervals throughout the day.[20] The robbers, identified by James Craig as "the Curry gang", remained just out of pistol range.[21] Craig was familiar with them from his days as manager of the VVV Cattle Company, said the outlaws home ground was "the Hole-in-the-Wall." The **Belle Fourche Times** issue of July 8, 1897 was the first time "the Hole-in-the-Wall" was used in print to describe one of the most famous outlaw havens in the west.[22]

James T. Craig, first to identify the bank robbers as "the Curry Gang", knew of the outlaws from his days as a Wyoming ranch manager. *(Photo: Courtesy Tri-State Museum, Belle Fourche, South Dakota.)*

Back in Belle Fource a large mob of irate citizens had gathered around O'Day and displayed a rope and every intention of hanging him. Safely in the protective clutches of the law O'Day taunted, "Go ahead and hang me, boys. You will never see a man die any gamer than I will."[23]

A few days earlier a one-legged man, arrested for being drunk, had started a fire in the jail to keep warm. He had such great success in his endeavor to keep warm that the jail, with the exception of the steel cage burned to the ground. Soon after the cage had cooled down he was again placed in the steel cage and given a day and night for meditation. After showing proper gratitude for not being lynched he was released on the condition he "quit" Belle Fourche; a condition he readily accepted. O'Day was the next illustrious "boarder" of the steel cage, remaining in it until the train was ready to leave Belle Fourche for Deadwood. After he was transferred to the Deadwood jail O'Day obtained W. O. Temple as his defense attorney.[24]

The preliminary hearing was scheduled to be held in Belle Fourche the next day. Butte County States Attorney T. W. La Fleiche advised Temple to waive the hearing and expressed his concern that, regardless of the outcome, O'Day would be lynched. Despite LaFleiche's advice Temple and his client showed up for the hearing. When it became necessary to postpone the hearing until the next day what to do with O'Day became an immediate problem. O'Day spent the night in the one place in Belle Fourche even he could attest to being impregnable — the vault of the Butte County Bank.[25]

After the testimony of eight of the twelve witnesses sworn in, Temple had heard enough and asked that the court pronounce its judgment. Justice C. T. Martin found sufficient evidence to hold O'Day for trial and set his bail in the amount of $15,000.[26] Just at the close of the examination Col. Parker announced that the remainder of the gang had been captured. "But as he was more than 'half seas over'," no one credited the erroneous report.[27]

Later, however, the rest of gang were captured by Montana man-hunters Jones D. Hicks and W. E. Smith near Red Lodge, Montana. "Kid" Curry, who was not one of the Butte County Bank robbers but was wanted elsewhere, escaped. Handcuffed together they gave the officers who returned them no trouble; not even "the Jones boys", who the **Queen City Mail** noted "seem to try to be ugly."[28]

On Halloween night all of the bank robbers, plus William Moore who was being held for murdering another man for mistreating a dog, escaped.[29] When the news of the jail escape reached Belle Fourche counselor Temple was advised that the remark, "After we catch the robbers, we ought to hang them on the spot, and then hang their lawyers afterwards," was being freely bandied about town.[30]

Tom O'Day and Walter Punteney, the only member of the gang to reform after the robbery[31], were soon recaptured near Spearfish. They were almost willing prisoners; they had not eaten for two days and their attempt to steal a horse was met with laughter when the horseman learned they were unarmed.[32] None of the other members of the gang were ever brought to trial for their part in the Butte County Bank robbery.

A change of venue was granted when twenty-seven of thirty persons interviewed by the court testified they could not obtain a fair trial in Butte County.[33] The trials, held in Deadwood, were bizarre — to say the least. The **Deadwood Independent**'s court reporter was an active worker for the defense. After each day's proceedings lawyer W.

Name........Harry Longbaugh, alias "Kid" Longbaugh, alias Harry Alonzo alias Frank Jones, alias Frank Boyd, alias the "Sundance Kid"

Nationality.......Swedish-American.. *Occupation*..............Cowboy; rustler

Criminal Occupation ....Highwayman, bank burglar, cattle and horse thief

Age........35 years............................... ...5 feet 10 in

Weight....165 to 175 lbs...........*Height*............................ Good

Eyes......Blue or gray..............*Build*.............................. ....Medium

Mustache or Beard...............*Complexion*..............(if any), natural color brown, reddish tinge

Features.....Grecian type.....*Nose*...........................Rather long

Color of Hair........Natural color brown, may be dyed ; combs it pompadour.

IS BOW-LEGGED AND HIS FEET FAR APART.

Remarks:—Harry Longbaugh served 18 months in jail at Sundance, Cook Co., Wyoming, when a boy, for horse stealing. In December, 1892, Harry Long- baugh, Bill Madden and Henry Bass "held up" a Great Northern train at Malta, Montana. Bass and Madden were tried for this crime, convicted and sentenced to 10 and 14 years respectively; Longbaugh escaped and since has been a fugitive. June 28, 1897, under the name of Frank Jones, Long- baugh participated with Harvey Logan, alias Curry, Tom Day and Walter Putney, in the Belle Fourche, South Dakota, bank robbery. All were ar- rested, but Longbaugh and Harvey Logan escaped from jail at Deadwood, October 31, the same year. Longbaugh has not since been arrested.

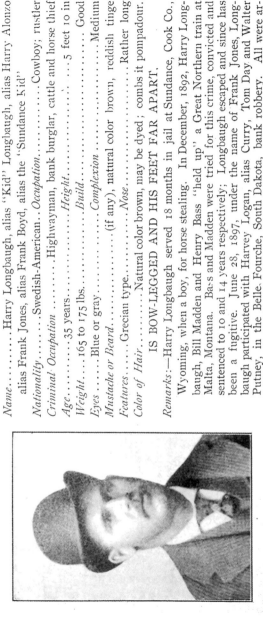

HARRY LONGBAUGH.

Photograph taken Nov. 21, 1900.

We also publish below a photograph, history and description of CAMILLA HANKS, alias O. C. HANKS, alias CHARLEY JONES, alias "DEAF" CHARLEY, who may be found in the company of either PARKER, alias CASSIDY or LONGBAUGH, alias ALONZO, and for whom a proportionate amount of a **$5,000.00 Reward** is offered by the GREAT NORTHERN EXPRESS COMPANY upon arrest and convic- tion for participation in the Great Northern (Railway) Express robbery near Wagner, Mont., July 3rd, 1901.

Inset of photo and information from Pinkerton National Detective Agency reward poster circulated January 24, 1902. Note that the information incorrectly identifies "Kid Curry" as one of the Butte County Bank robbers. It also identifies "The Sundance Kid" as "one of the Jones boys who seem to try to be ugly." It identifies Tom O'Day as Tom Day. *(Photo: Courtesy Wyoming State Archives, Museums, and Historical Department.)*

O. Temple donned a reporter's attire and reported for the **Pioneer-Times**. Editor A. D. Shockley of the **Belle Fourche Times** candidly admitted that he found Temple's reporting "quite affecting (to the stomach)" and commented on the manner in which reporter Temple marveled at the courtroom genius of lawyer Temple.[34]

Punteney was placed on trial first and was found not guilty of participation in the bank robbery. He was then placed on trial for assault with a deadly weapon for his part in shooting up and down the

street during the robbery. To this charge Punteney pleaded self-defense; an interesting plea since he had been found not guilty of being involved in the bank robbery.[35] After the trial all members of the jury, the judge, and the attorneys were asked to assume the places they had maintained during the trial. Miss Nellie, Walter's sister, wanted a photograph.[36]

Walter Punteney, the only member of the gang to reform. Punteney later worked in Buffalo Bill's "Wild West Show" and owned a bar in Pinedale, Wyoming. Punteney died at Pinedale, April 19, 1950. *(Photo: Courtesy Wyoming Archives, Museums and Historical Dept.)*

It was felt that a better case had been made against O'Day and that at least one of the robbers would get a prison sentence. Not long into the trial it could be seen that, in spite of the evidence, O'Day would also be found not guilty.[37] O'Day and Punteney were then indicted for the escape Halloween night. On a motion by Lawrence County States Attorney Wilson the indictment was set aside. Wilson felt that he could not prove O'Day and Punteney had actually escaped, but perhaps had "walked out when the way was clear as many innocent man, yielding to impulse and love of freedom has done before." It was an understandable argument. That was precisely what Temple had maintained had happened all along.[38]

Tom O'Day soon became the idol of a curious matinee drinking crowd at Carter's Resort in Deadwood which prompted **Times** editor Shockley to think that O'Day's future might hold bigger and better

things in store for him. He imagined O'Day upon a pedestal in a
Chicago dime museum with a placard bearing the inscription:

Prof. LeDay, the only living white human being who
ever invaded the sacred city of Belle Fourche. Kept a prisoner
for twenty-seven weeks by the man eating natives. Photos 10
cents.[39]

However, Buffalo Bill nor the museum managers ever called and
by April O'Day's departure from Deadwood was scarcely newsworthy. "Tom O'Day . . . left last evening for the central part of
Wyoming, where he will probably go to work on the range again as a
cowboy."[40]

1.   Denis McLoughlin, **Wild and Woolly; An Encyclopedia of the Old
      West**, pp. 376-377.
2.   Op. Cit., pp. 102-103.
3.   **Belle Fourche Times**, July 8, 1897.
4.   **Deadwood Pioneer-Times**, July 29, 1897.
5.   Butte County Court Records. "Evidence taken before C. T. Martin,
      Justice of the Peace, in the Case of the State of South Dakota vs.
      Thomas O'Day," (hereinafter referred to as Evidence), p. 7, Belle
      Fourche, South Dakota.
6.   **Belle Fourche Times**, July 1, 1897.
7.   Charles Kelly, **The Outlaw Trail; The Story of Butch Cassidy and
      "The Wild Bunch"**, p. 122, Bonanza, N.Y., 1958; related the story as
      to by Sheriff Sproule of Johnson County, Wyoming.
8.   **Deadwood Pioneer-Times**, June 29, 1897.
9.   Ibid.
10.   Butte County Court Records. "Evidence", op. cit., p. 7; "Informa-
      tion for Robbery"; Belle Fourche.
11.   **Deadwood Pioneer-Times**, op. cit. A local legend that finds its way
      into print occasionally is that Tom O'Day rode into Belle Fourche
      "on a scout", and became intoxicated. When the "scout" did not
      return, the rest of the gang were in the process of robbing the bank
      without him, and O'Day awakened, ran out of the saloon (sometimes
      a box car), and was promptly captured. Court records and contem-
      porary accounts indicate this is nothing but local legend.
12.   Evidence, op. cit., p. 6.
13.   Evidence, op. cit., p. 10.
14.   Ibid.
15.   **Deadwood Pioneer-Times; Belle Fourche Times**, op. cit.
16.   **Belle Fourche Times**, op. cit.
17.   **Queen City Mail**, Spearfish, S.D., June 30, 1897.
18.   Evidence, op. cit., pp. 7 and 11.
19.   Evidence, op. cit., p. 9
20.   **Deadwood Pioneer-Times**, op. cit.; **Queen City Mail**, June 30, 1897.
21.   **Queen City Mail**, July 7, 1897.
22.   **Belle Fourche Times**, July 8, 1897.
23.   **Deadwood Pioneer-Times**, op. cit.
24.   **Belle Fourche Times**, July 1, 1897.

25. Butte County Court Records. Affadavit of W. O. Temple; Affadavit of Frankie McGregor; Belle Fourche. **Deadwood Pioneer-Times**, op. cit.
26. Butte County Court Records. "Action for Robbery", issued June 29, 1897, Belle Fourche.
27. **Sturgis Weekly Record**, October 1, 1897; **Queen City Mail**, September 29, October 6, 1897; **Belle Fourche Times**, op. cit.
28. **Queen City Mail**, October 6, 1897.
29. **Sturgis Weekly Record**, November 5, 1897.
30. Butte County Court Records. "Affadavit of Frankie McGregor". Belle Fourche.
31. Pinkerton Report, Denver Criminal Division, History #1728, Walter Putney. The correct spelling is Punteney, which was noted in one issue of the **Pioneer-Times**, who, knowing the difference, spelled it Putney anyway. **Portrait and Biographical History of Marshall County** (Kansas); 1889; Chapman Bros.; Chicago; pp. 700-703 spells the family name Punteney in giving a biographical sketch of Eli Punteney, Walter's father.
32. **Queen City Mail**, November 3, 1897.
33. Butte County Court Records, "Journal", March Term, 1898. Belle Fourche.
34. **Belle Fourche Times**, March 31, 1898; **Queen City Mail**, April 6, 1898.
35. **Deadwood Pioneer-Times**, April 13, 1898; **Queen City Mail**, March 20, April 14, 1898.
36. **Deadwood Pioneer-Times**, April 2, 1898.
37. **Belle Fourche Times**, March 31, 1898.
38. **Deadwood Pioneer-Times**, March 24, 1898; Lawrence County Court Records. Order by Judge Plowman. Deadwood.
39. **Belle Fourche Times**, March 10, 1898.
40. **Belle Fourche Times**, April 28, 1898.

THE END OF THEIR ERA

The train, its whistle echoing up the canyon, signalled the end of the era to which the stagemen belonged. Most "hung up their guns" and lived in harmony with the progress that brought the iron horse. W. B. "Bat" Masterson, although not identified with the stage lines of the Black Hills and Wyoming, spoke for a legion of displaced messengers everywhere when he turned down the U.S. Marshalship of Indian Territory: "I'd have some drunken boy to kill once a year. Some kid who was born after I took my guns off would get drunk and look me over; and the longer he looked the less he'd be able to see where my reputation came from. In the end he'd crawl 'round to gun play and I'd have to send him over the jump. Almost any other man could hold the office and never see a moment's trouble. But I couldn't . . ."[1] Some of the messengers became lawmen and Bat's prophecy, in a few instances, came true: Fred Willard killed Roy Sewell in Sturgis; Jesse Brown was a member of the last posse Jack Sully tried to elude; Scott Davis and Jack Flagg were only prevented from killing each other by bystanders.

The personal tragedy of Boone May was that he had outlived the era to which he belonged, and it passed into history before his eyes. Just as the establishment of courts had taken his silent, solitary outlaw stalking expeditions from him, the treasure chests that he risked his life to protect fell victim to the train. Boone and men like him moved on, to the Klondike gold rush, to South America, to anywhere they could find life lived as they knew it. The ever present danger was their lifeblood. Staying in the face of progress would have been as fatal to these men as any bullet ever molded. Death found Boone May in

South America, and the others elsewhere, but they had added years to their lives by going.

The **Bald Mountain News** recalled and updated the lives of the "historic eight" in 1899:

> . . . There were eight of the organized messengers: Jesse Brown, Jim Brown, Scott Davis, Ross Davis, Boon (sic) May, Bill May, Billy Sample, and Gale Hill. Rafferty, who accidentally shot himself while getting out of the coach,[2] was employed as an extra. Of the eight messengers who made history on the Cheyenne-Deadwood stage route, Jesse Brown is the only one remaining in the Black Hills. Gale Hill died several years ago from the effect of a gun shot wound received in a fight with road agents in Cold Springs,[3] when Campbell, the telegraph operator was killed. Jim Brown died in Arizona. Bill May was killed in Toson (sic), Arizona, by a tough with whom he had some trouble at Sidney, Neb., several years before meeting in Arizona. Boone May died of malaria in South America. Scott Davis is in Utah traveling for a commission house. His brother Ross is living on a Nebraska sheep ranch. Billy Sample is a Wells-Fargo messenger on a Mexican railroad. Billy Sample and Ross Davis never smelt powder during their term of service with the Cheyenne and Black Hills Stage Co., but would have stood fire. The other six were in several engagements with road agents. Scott Davis was the captain and the bulldog fighter; Jim Brown was the quicker on the trigger; Boone May was on the shoot with or without provacation, yet he was a small blonde, mild-mannered and speechy. Jesse Brown and Gale Hill never looked for trouble, they avoided it so far as consistent, but when it came they would stand up and shoot and be shot at without flinching.[4]

Many of the outlaws emerged from prison to a world that had passed them by. They worked as hard to catch up as they had ridden from posses. Some had not lived to see the new era, and perhaps it was best they didn't. Among them would have been many who would have died slow, day-by-day deaths in prison, or committed suicide. Those who died had played against the odds and lost — but they had met death on their terms, not someone else's. Some, men like Jim Mc-Cloud, continued to live outside the law for the rest of their lives, but they were a minority. None emerged from prison and attempted to re-create the world as it had been. It was men like Tom Vernon, Ed Harrington, and Bill Carlisle who later made headlines by robbing trains and stages. They were poor imitators of the men who had preceded them.

1. -------, "William Barclay (Bat) Masterson," **Human Life,** January, 1907, p. 10.
2. William Rafferty was accidentally shot when a revolver fell out of his hands and struck the brake. The gun fired and Rafferty was "almost instantly killed," January 22, 1879. **(Black Hills Daily Times,** January 22, 1879.)
3. Canyon Springs.
4. **Bald Mountain News,** January 6, 1899.

ACKNOWLEDGEMENTS

There has never been a volume devoted exclusively to the outlaws of the Black Hills and Wyoming. Previously the outlaws of the area have been relegated to chapters of books concerning both the Black Hills and Wyoming, biographies and autobiographies of men who knew them, chased them, and captured them. While most books that dealt with this area in some way had material about the outlaws of the Black Hills and Wyoming, bits of information can also be found about them in books like **Folklore of Highland County** (Ohio), **Dodge City,** and **Legends of the California Bandidos.** Some, Jim McCloud for instance, could only be found as a footnote to the more famous, or infamous, Tom Horn.

To say that the contemporary newsmen had little regard for the proper spelling of their names would be an understatement. "Duck" Goodale became "Dug" or "Doug" Goodale; Dunc Blackburn became "Doc" Blackburn; and there was little effort to separate the various "kids" from one another. Often the participants became recognizable only through the relating of an event. The many "fifty years in the saddle" books were of great value in providing the original lead to a story, but at the same time I was amazed at how often "Wild Bill," "California Joe," and "Calamity Jane" came out of the grave to ride with the cowboys and talk to the miners about rich forgotten claims. It could have been nothing short of divine providence that only those who later wrote their memoirs were selected for their guidance.

I would estimate that over the past ten years I have received answers to over one thousand queries. Without those hundreds of Federal, State, and county employees across the United States, the many librarians, historical societies, and others, this book could never have been written. I thank each one for the time they took to answer my letters.

Those especially helpful were: John Carter and the late Paul D. Riley, Nebraska Historical Society; Larry Jochims and Christie Stanley, Kansas State Historical Society; Catherine T. Engel, Colorado Historical Society; Barry B. Combs, Union Pacific Railroad; Barbara Bush, Arizona Historical Society; Mrs. Mary Belle Lambertson, Carbon County Museum; Mrs. Bess Sheller, Carbon County Library; the Montana Historical Society; the Miles City Public Library; and the Denver Public Library, Western History Department.

Special thanks to Mrs. Ida Wozny, Mrs. Paula West, and Mrs. Jean Brainerd, of the Wyoming State Archives, Museums, and Historical Department; Emmett D. Chisum and Mrs. Paula McDougal, American Heritage Center, University of Wyoming; Dayton Canaday and Bonnie Gardner, South Dakota Historical Resource Center, and the following Black Hills area librarians: Carol Davis and staff, Sturgis Public Library; Marjorie Pontius and staff, Carnegie Library, Deadwood; Edith Wood and staff, Grace Balloch Memorial Library, Spearfish; Mrs. Jean Diggins, Reference Librarian, Rapid City Public Library. Also to South Dakota State Library Interlibrary Loans Librarians Delores Jorgensen, Connie Scofield, and Selma Dunham; South Dakota State Library Reference Librarians; and Pat Engebretson, Helen Herrett, Voncille Kirkpatrick, Kay Heck and Aileen Montgomery (retired), of the Belle Fourche Public Library.

To Otto Engebretson for the many times he picked up the phone to hear a voice on the other end say, "I've got a 'technical problem' I need help with," and guiding me through, usually the inaccuracies, of how I wanted to word something.

To Pat Engebretson, Tom and Rae Ann Trotter, Aileen Montgomery, and Judi Douglass for suggestions, proofreading, and saving me from the embarrassment of participles that dangled.

To Otto, Steve, and Candy for letting me live in my world of outlaws while they played, for the most part, quietly. Perhaps a more disciplined person really can write under almost any conditions. I have never been accused of being disciplined, let alone that disciplined.

And to Pat for financial support for the past seven months, with only occasional lapses into martyrdom, and who knew the difference between lying around and writing, and nudged me when the former exceeded the latter.

Doug Engebretson
813½ Day
Belle Fourche, S.D.

BIBLIOGRAPHY

Books

Adams, Ramon Frederick. BURS UNDER THE SADDLE. Norman: University of Oklahoma Press, 1964.

-----. MORE BURS UNDER THE SADDLE. Norman: University of Oklahoma Press, 1979.

-----. SIX-GUNS AND SADDLE LEATHER. Norman: University of Oklahoma Press, 1st Edition, 1954.

-----. SIX-GUNS AND SADDLE LEATHER. Norman: University of Oklahoma Press, 2nd Edition, 1969.

-----. WESTERN WORDS, Norman: University of Oklahoma Press, 1968.

Allen, W. C. THE ANNALS OF HAYWOOD COUNTY, NORTH CAROLINA, 1808-1935. n.p. 1935.

American Guide Series. A SOUTH DAKOTA GUIDE. New York: Hastings House, 1952.

-----. WYOMING. New York: Oxford University Press, 1941.

Anonymous. BANDITTI OF THE ROCKY MOUNTAINS AND VIGILANCE COMMITTEE IN IDAHO. Minneapolis: Ross & Haines, Inc., 1964.

Athearn, Robert G. UNION PACIFIC COUNTRY. Lincoln: University of Nebraska Press. 1976.

Ayres, Elsie Johnson. THE HILLS OF HIGHLAND. Springfield, Ohio: H. K. Skinner & Sons, 1971.

Baker, Pearl. THE WILD BUNCH AT ROBBERS ROOST. Los Angeles: Westernlore Press, 1965.

Bennett, Estelline. OLD DEADWOOD DAYS. New York: J. H. Sears & Co., Inc., 1928.

Black, A. P. (Ott). THE END OF THE LONG HORN TRAIL. Selfridge, N.D.: Selfridge Journal, n.d.

Bourke, John G. ON THE BORDER WITH CROOK. Lincoln: University of Nebraska Press, 1971.

Bragg, William F., Jr. WYOMING: RUGGED BUT RIGHT. Boulder, Co.: Pruett Publishing, 1979.

Bridwell, J. W. THE LIFE AND ADVENTURES OF ROBERT MCKIMIE, ALIAS "LITTLE REDDY," FROM TEXAS. Hillsboro, Ohio: Hillsboro Gazette, 1878.

Bronson, Edgar Beecher. RED BLOODED. Chicago: A. C. McClurg, 1910.

-----. THE VANGUARD. New York: George H. Doran Co., 1914.

Brown, Dee. BURY MY HEART AT WOUNDED KNEE. New York: Bantam Books, 1972.

Brown, Jesse & A. M. Willard. THE BLACK HILLS TRAILS. Rapid City: Rapid City Journal, 1924.

Brown, Mark H. and W. R. Felton. THE FRONTIER YEARS. New York: Henry Holt & Co., 1955.

Bryan, Jerry. AN ILLINOIS GOLD HUNTER IN THE BLACK HILLS. Springfield, ILL.: Illinois State Historical Society, 1960.

Burroughs, John Rolfe. WHERE THE OLD WEST STAYED YOUNG. New York: Bonanza Books, 1962.

Burt, Maxwell Struthers. POWDER RIVER: LET 'ER BUCK. New York: Farrar & Rinehart, Inc., 1938.

Bye, John O. BACKTRAILING IN THE HEART OF THE SHORT-GRASS COUNTRY. Published by author, 1956.

Canton, Frank M. FRONTIER TRAILS. Norman: University of Oklahoma Press, 1966.

Casey, Robert J. THE BLACK HILLS AND THEIR INCREDIBLE CHARACTERS. Indianapolis: Bobbs-Merrill, 1949.

Clay, John. MY LIFE ON THE RANGE. Chicago: Privately printed, 1924.

Collier, William Ross & Edwin Victor Westrate. DAVE COOK OF THE ROCKIES. New York: Rufus Rockwell Wilson, Inc., 1936.

Cowan, Robert Ellsworth (Bub). RANGE RIDER. Garden City, N.Y.: Doubleday, Doran & Co., 1930.

Crawford, Lewis Ferandus. REKINDLING CAMP FIRES. Bismarck: Capital Book Co., 1926.

Cory, Homer. CORN COUNTRY. New York: Duell, Sloan and Pearce, 1947.

David, Robert Beebe, MALCOLM CAMPBELL, SHERIFF. Casper, Wyo.: Wyomingana, 1932.

Driscoll, R. E. SEVENTY YEARS OF BANKING IN THE BLACK HILLS. Rapid City: Gate City Guide, 1948.

Elman, Robert. BADMEN OF THE WEST. n.p.: Ridge Press, 1974.

Fatout, Paul. AMBROSE BIERCE AND THE BLACK HILLS. Norman: University of Oklahoma Press, 1956.

Fielder, Mildred. WILD BILL AND DEADWOOD. Seattle: Superior, 1965.

Finerty, John F. (Milo Milton Quaife, ed.) WAR PATH AND BIVOUAC. Lincoln: University of Nebraska Press, 1966.

Fisher, Vardis & Opal Laurel Holmes. GOLD RUSHES AND MINING CAMPS OF THE EARLY AMERICAN WEST. Caldwell, Idaho: Caxton Printers, 1968.

Flannery, L. G. (Pat), ed. JOHN HUNTON'S DIARY. VOLS. 1-5. Lingle, Wyo.: Guide-Review, 1958-1964.

-----. JOHN HUNTON'S DIARY, VOL. 6. Glendale, Ca.: Arthur H. Clark Company, 1970.

Freeman, James W., ed. PROSE AND POETRY OF LIVE STOCK INDUSTRY OF THE UNITED STATES . . . . Denver and Kansas City: Franklin Hudson Publishing Co., 1905.

Gard, Wayne. SAM BASS. Boston: Houghton Mifflin Co., 1936.

Gordon, S. RECOLLECTIONS OF OLD MILESTOWN. Miles City, MT.: Independent Printing Co., 1918.

Hagedorn, Hermann. ROOSEVELT IN THE BAD LANDS. Boston: Houghton Mifflin Co., 1930.

Hebert, Frank. 40 YEARS PROSPECTING AND MINING IN THE BLACK HILLS OF SOUTH DAKOTA. Rapid City: Rapid City Journal, 1921.

Hening, H. B., ed. GEORGE CURRY, 1861-1947. Albuquerque: University of New Mexico, 1958.

Hendricks, George David. THE BAD MEN OF THE WEST. San Antonio: Naylor Co., 1941.

HISTORY OF ADAIR COUNTY, IOWA. Adair County Historical Society, 1976.

HISTORY OF MONTANA, 1739-1885. Chicago: Warner, Beers, & Co., 1885.

Homsher, Lola M., ed. SOUTH PASS, 1868. Lincoln: University of Nebraska Press, 1960.

Horn, Tom. LIFE OF TOM HORN. Norman: University of Oklahoma Press, 1964.

Hoyt, Henry Franklin. A FRONTIER DOCTOR. Boston: Houghton Mifflin Co., 1929.

Hughes, Richard B. (Agnes Wright Spring, ed.) PIONEER YEARS IN THE BLACK HILLS. Glendale, Ca.: Arthur H. Clark Co., 1957.

Huidekoper, Wallis. LAND OF THE DACOTAHS. Helena: Montana Stockgrowers Association, 1949.

Hutton, Harold. DOC MIDDLETON. Chicago: Swallow Press, 1974.

Karolevitz, Robert F. YANKTON: A PIONEER PAST. Aberdeen, SD: North Plains Press, 1977.

Kellar, Kenneth C. SETH BULLOCK: FRONTIER MARSHAL. Aberdeen, SD: North Plains Press, 1972.

Kelly, Charles. THE OUTLAW TRAIL. New York: Devin-Adair Co., 1959.

Krakel, Dean F. THE SAGA OF TOM HORN. Laramie, Wyo.: Powder River Publishers, 1954.

Kuykendall, William Littlebury. FRONTIER DAYS. n.p.: J. M. & H. J. Kuykendall, publishers, 1917.

Lake, Stuart N. WYATT EARP, FRONTIER MARSHAL. Boston: Houghton Mifflin Co., 1931.

Larson, T. A. HISTORY OF WYOMING. Lincoln: University of Nebraska Press, 1965.

Lathrop, George. SOME PIONEER RECOLLECTIONS. Philadelphia: George W. Jacobs & Co., 1927.

Lee, Bob, ed. GOLD-GALS-GUNS-GUTS. Deadwood, SD: Deadwood-Lead '76 Centennial, Inc., 1976.

Leedy, Carl. BLACK HILLS PIONEER STORIES. Lead, SD: Bonanza Trails Publications, 1973.

-----. GOLDEN DAYS IN THE BLACK HILLS. n.p. n.d.

LeFors, Joe. WYOMING PEACE OFFICER. Laramie, Wyo.: Laramie Printing Co., 1953.

McClintock, John S. PIONEER DAYS IN THE BLACK HILLS. Deadwood, SD: Published by Author, 1939.

McGillycuddy, Julia B. MCGILLYCUDDY, AGENT. Stanford University Press, 1941.

McLoughlin, Denis. WILD & WOOLLY. Garden City, N.Y.: Doubleday, 1975.

McPherren, Ida (Mrs. Geneva Gibson). EMPIRE BUILDERS. Sheridan, Wyo.: Star Publishing Co., 1942.

Martin, Charles Lee. A SKETCH OF SAM BASS, THE BANDIT. Norman: University of Oklahoma Press, 1956.

Mattison, Ray H. ROOSEVELT AND THE STOCKMEN'S ASSOCIATION. Bismarck, N.D.: State Historical Society of North Dakota, 1950.

Mercer, Asa Shinn. THE BANDITTI OF THE PLAINS. Norman: University of Oklahoma Press, 1954.

Miller, Nina Hull. SHUTTERS WEST. Denver: Sage Books, 1962.

Milner, Joe E., and Earle F. Forrest. CALIFORNIA JOE, NOTED SCOUT AND INDIAN FIGHTER. Caldwell, Idaho: Caxton Printers, 1935.

Mokler, Alfred James. HISTORY OF NATRONA COUNTY, WYOMING, 1888-1922. Chicago: R. R. Donnelley & Sons Co., 1923.

Monaghan, Jay, ed. THE BOOK OF THE AMERICAN WEST. New York: Julian Messner, 1963.

Morgan, Violet. FOLKLORE OF HIGHLAND COUNTY. Greenfield, Ohio: Greenfield Printing & Publishing Co., 1946.

Nash, Jay Robert. BLOODLETTERS AND BADMEN. New York: M. Evans and Company, Inc., 1973.

100 YEARS IN THE WILD WEST: A PICTORIAL HISTORY OF RAWLINS, WYOMING. Rawlins: Times Stationers, 1968.

O'Reilly, Harrington. FIFTY YEARS ON THE TRAIL. Norman: University of Oklahoma Press, 1963.

Parker, Watson. DEADWOOD: THE GOLDEN YEARS. Lincoln: University of Nebraska Press, 1981.

-----. GOLD IN THE BLACK HILLS. Norman: University of Oklahoma Press, 1966.

Parkhill, Forbes. THE WILDEST OF THE WEST. New York: Henry Holt & CO., 1951.

Pence, Mary Lou & Lola M. Homsher. THE GHOST TOWNS OF WYOMING. New York: Hastings House, 1956.

Pinkerton, William A. TRAIN ROBBERIES, TRAIN ROBBERS AND THE "HOLD UP" MEN. Fort Davis, Texas: Frontier Book Co., 1968.

Raine, William MacLeod. GUNS OF THE FRONTIER. Boston: Houghton Mifflin, 1940.

Rankin, M. Wilson. REMINISCENCES OF FRONTIER DAYS, INCLUDING AN AUTHENTIC ACCOUNT OF THE THORNBURG AND MEEKER MASSACRE. Denver: Smith-Brooks, 1938.

Rezatto, Helen. MOUNT MORIAH: "KILL A MAN—START A CEMETERY." Aberdeen, SD: North Plains Press, 1980.

Rickards, Colin. MYSTERIOUS DAVE MATHERS. Santa Fe: Press of the Territorian, 1968.

Robinson, Doane. DOANE ROBINSON'S ENCYCLOPEDIA OF SOUTH DAKOTA. Pierre, SD: Published by author, 1925.

Rosa, Joseph G. THE GUNFIGHTER, MAN OR MYTH. Norman: University of Oklahoma Press, 1969.

----. THEY CALLED HIM WILD BILL. Norman: University of Oklahoma Press, 1964.

Rosen, Rev. Peter. PA-HA-SA-PAH: OR, THE BLACK HILLS OF SOUTH DAKOTA. St. Louis: Nixon-Jones Printing Co., 1895.

Rynning, Thomas Harbo. GUN NOTCHES. New York: Frederick A. Stokes Co., 1931.

Sanders, Helen Fitzgerald. X. BEIDLER, VIGILANTE. Norman: University of Oklahoma Press, 1957.

Scott, George W. THE BLACK HILLS STORY. Fort Collins, Co.: Published by author, 1953.

Smith, Helena Huntington. THE WAR ON POWDER RIVER. Lincoln: University of Nebraska Press, 1967.

Sneve, Virginia Driving Hawk (ed.). SOUTH DAKOTA GEOGRAPHIC NAMES. Sioux Falls: Brevet Press, 1973.

Spring, Agnes Wright. THE CHEYENNE AND BLACK HILLS STAGE AND EXPRESS ROUTES. Glendale, Ca.: Arthur H. Clark Co., 1949.

-----, ed. PIONEER YEARS IN THE BLACK HILLS (See Hughes).

Sweetman, Luke D. BACK TRAILING ON THE OPEN RANGE. Caldwell, Idaho: Caxton Printers, 1951.

Sundstrom, Jessie Y., ed. CUSTER COUNTY HISTORY TO 1976. Custer, SD: Custer County Historical Society, 1977.

Swallow, Alan, ed. THE WILD BUNCH. Denver: Sage Books, 1966.

Tallent, Annie D. THE BLACK HILLS; OR, THE LAST HUNTING GROUND OF THE DAKOTAHS. Sioux Falls: Brevet Press, 1974.

Trenholm, Virginia Cole. FOOTPRINTS ON THE FRONTIER. Douglas, Wyo.: Douglas Enterprise Co., 1945.

Urbanek, Mae. GHOST TRAILS OF WYOMING. Boulder, Co.: Johnson Publishing Company, 1978.

----- and Jerry Urbanek. KNOW WYOMING. Boulder, Co.: Johnson Publishing, 1969.

Vestal, Stanley. QUEEN OF COWTOWNS, DODGE CITY. New York: Harper & Brothers, 1952.

Voorhees, Luke. PERSONAL RECOLLECTIONS OF PIONEER LIFE ON THE MOUNTAINS AND PLAINS OF THE GREAT WEST. Cheyenne, Wyo.: Privately printed, 1920.

Walker, Tacetta B. STORIES OF EARLY DAYS IN WYOMING: BIG HORN BASIN. Caspar, Wyo.: Prairie Publishing Co.

WATER RESOURCES SURVEY: PRAIRIE COUNTY MONTANA, PART I. Helena: Montana Water Resources Board, 1970.

Webb, Walter Prescott (ed.). THE HANDBOOK OF TEXAS. Austin: Texas State Historical Association, 1952, VOL. 2.

Wellman, Paul I. A DYNASTY OF WESTERN OUTLAWS. Garden City, N.Y.: Doubleday & CO., 1961.

Westerners' Brand Book (Denver Posse). 1945 BRAND BOOK. Denver: Westerners, 1946.

-----. 1948 BRAND BOOK. Denver: Artcraft Press, 1949.

White, Russell H. HISTORICAL REVIEW OF THE WOODBURY COUNTY SHERIFF'S DEPARTMENT. Sioux City: Russell H. White, 1981.

Wyman, Walker D. NOTHING BUT PRAIRIE AND SKY. Norman: University of Oklahoma Press, 1954.

Wyoming Recreation Commission. WYOMING: A GUIDE TO HISTORIC SITES. Basin, Wyoming: Big Horn Publishers, 1976.

Young, Harry (Sam). HARD KNOCKS. Portland, Oregon: Wells and Co., 1915.

Articles

Anderson, Harry H. "An Account of Deadwood and the Northern Black Hills in 1876," SOUTH DAKOTA HISTORICAL COLLECTIONS. Vol. 31 (1962), pp. 287-364.

Bailey, C. J. "Lights and Shades of a Strenuous Career," DACOTAH MAGAZINE (July, 1908), pp. 1-10.

Bushfield, J. A. "An Incident of the Black Hills Holdup," MONTHLY SOUTH DAKOTAN, Vol. II, #2 (June, 1899).

Collins, Dabney Otis. "Skin Game in Wyoming," EMPIRE MAGAZINE (Nov. 17, 1974).

Condit, Thelma Gatchell. "The Hole-in-the-Wall," ANNALS OF WYOMING, Vol. 30, #1 (April, 1958), p. 35.

Cornell, Sidney. "The Opening of the Hills," MONTHLY SOUTH DAKOTAN, Vol. I, #10, #11.

"Death and a Pair of Shoes," ADVENTURE MAGAZINE (August, 1947).

"The Exit of Exelby," MONTHLY SOUTH DAKOTAN. Vol. 4, #2 (June, 1901), pp. 51-53.

Johnson, Dorothy M. "Durable Desperado Kid Curry," MONTANA: MAGAZINE OF WESTERN HISTORY, Vol. VI, #2, pp. 22-31.

Lyons, T. D. "Black Hills Freighter: Reminiscences from the Dakotas," COMMONWEAL, Vol. 35 (Dec. 19, 1941), pp. 216-19.

Mantz, Judge H. J. "Audubon County's 'Troublesome Gang,' " ANNUALS OF IOWA, Vol. 30 (1949-51), pp. 269-278.

Masterson, W. B. (Bat). "Famous Gun Fighters of the Western Frontier," HUMAN LIFE (January, 1907), pp. 9-10.

Meldrum, John W. "The Taming of 'Big Nosed George' — and others," UNION PACIFIC MAGAZINE (November, 1926), p. 8-9.

Metz, Leon C. "Hardin Called West's Most Dangerous Gunman," El Paso Times, August 20, 1972.

"The Montana Stranglers," TRUE WESTERN ADVENTURE (August, 1967), p. 31.

"Mrs. Sarah C. Bowman," THE TRAIL, Vol. 8, #4 (September, 1915), p. 27.

Richardson, Leander P. "A Trip to the Black Hills," SCRIBNER'S, Vol. XIII (April, 1977), pp. 748-56.

Spring, Agnes Wright. "Who Robbed the Mail Coach?" FRONTIER TIMES (September, 1967), pp. 25 + .

Wilson, William E. (Limestone), "Blizzards and Buffalo," MONTANA: A MAGAZINE OF WESTERN HISTORY, Vol. XIX, #1 (January, 1969), p. 38.

Newspapers

Atlantic (Iowa) Telegraph

Anaconda (Montana) Standard

Bald Mountain News (Terry, SD)

Bill Barlow's Budget (Douglas, Wyoming)

Bisbee (Arizona) Daily Review

Belle Fourche Times

Black Hills Central (Rochford)

Black Hills Daily Times (Deadwood)
Black Hills Journal (Rapid City)
Black Hills Pioneer (Deadwood)
Black Hills Weekly Times (Deadwood)
Central City (Nebraska) Courier
Cheyenne Daily Leader
Cheyenne Daily Sun
Custer County (South Dakota) Chronicle
Fairfield (Montana) Times
Grant County (Kansas) Republican
Great Falls (Montana) Tribune
Helena (Montana) Weekly Herald
Judith Basin (Montana) County Press
Judith Gap (Montana) Journal
Kearney (Nebraska) Press
Lusk (Wyoming) Herald
Miles City (Montana) Daily Press
Omaha (Nebraska) Republican
Queen City Mail (Spearfish, SD)
Rawlins (Wyoming) Daily Times
Rawlins (Wyoming) Republican
Rawlins (Wyoming) Republican and Wyoming Reporter
Santa Fe New Mexican
Sturgis Weekly Record
Topeka (Kansas) Daily Capital
Waverly (Ohio) Watchman
Wyoming Derrick (Casper, Wyoming)
Yankton Press & Dakotian
Yellowstone Journal (Miles City, Montana)

Prison Records and Related Material

Prison Records Books, Wyoming State Archives, Museums and Historical Department, Cheyenne, Wyoming:
  Duncan Blackburn
  James Dale
  Edward Mewis

James McCloud

James Wall

Prison Records, United States Penitentiary, Leavenworth, Kansas:
Jim William McCloud

Prison Records, Federal Correctional Institution, Seagoville, Texas:
Jim William McCloud

Related

Pinkerton Report, Denver Criminal Division, History #1728, Walter
Putney (sic)

Court Records:

Butte County Court Records. State of South Dakota vs. George
Curry, Harve Ray, Thomas O'Day, Walter Punteney, Thomas
Jones, and Frank Jones. Butte County Courthouse, Belle Fourche,
SD.

Carbon County Court Records. Territory of Wyoming vs. George
Parrott, Testimony taken November 17, 1880. Typescript in Wyo-
ming State Archives, Museums, and Historical Department, Chey-
enne, Wyoming. Territory of Wyoming vs. George Parott alias Big
Nosed George Impleaded with Frank James alias McKinney Sim
Wan Et. al. Indictment for Murder. Loc. cit.

Converse County Court Records. State of Wyoming vs. Edward
Mewis. State of Wyoming vs. James Dale. Converse County Courthouse, Douglas, Wyoming.

Lawrence County Court Records. State of South Dakota vs. George
Curry, Harve Ray, Thomas O'Day, Walter Punteney, Thomas
Jones, Frank Jones. Lawrence County Courthouse, Deadwood,
South Dakota.

Manuscripts and Papers

Mrs. Thomas Blackburn Family Bible.

Peirce, Ellis Taylor. "Odd Characters and Incidents in the Black Hills
During the 70's." Typescript in the South Dakota Historical Resource Center, Pierre, SD.

South Dakota WPA Writer's Project, "Annals of Early Rapid City,
1878-1887: Crime." Typescript copy in Rapid City Public Library,
Rapid City, SD.

Tays Family Papers, Pans Manuscript Room, Public Archives of
Nova Scotia, Halifax, Nova Scotia.

Interviews

Edmo LeClair interviewed by M. L. Simpson, June 22, 1926. Typescript copy, Simpson Collection, American Heritage Center, University of Wyoming, Laramie, Wyoming.

Mrs. Margaret Lynch, Shubenacadie, East Hants County, Nova Scotia interviewed by Alma Mathews, Shubenacadie, East Hants County, Nova Scotia, June 14, 1980, for author.

Census, Indexes, and Directories:

1850 Iowa Federal Census (Wapello County)

1850 Pennsylvania Federal Census — Index

1864 Philadelphia City Directory

1870 Wyoming Territorial Census — Index

1870 Dakota Territory Census

1880 Wyoming Federal Census (Carbon County)

1880 Dakota Territory Federal Census (Lawrence County)

1912 Miles City (Montana) City Directory

Reports and Documents:

City of Philadelphia, Second Annual Report to the Directors of City Trusts, Philadelphia, Pennsylvania, January, 1872.

City of Philadelphia, Third Annual Report to the Directors of City Trusts, Philadelphia, Pennsylvania, 1873.

Certificate of Death, James William McCloud, #019733, State of Oklahoma, Department of Health, Oklahoma City, Oklahoma.

Letters to author

Carol Willsey Bell, C. G., Reference Archivist, Ohio Historical Society, Inc., Columbus, Ohio, June 18, 1980.

Ward J. Childs, Archivist III, Department of Records, City of Philadelphia, Philadelphia, Pennsylvania, February 7, 1980.

Forrest Daniel, Research Assistant, State Historical Society of North Dakota, January 26, 1978.

James Q. Donahue, Archivist/Historian, Wyoming State Archives, Museums, and Historical Department, Cheyenne, Wyoming, June 29, 1979.

Henry F. Hussey, Chief U.S. Probation Officer, Western District, Oklahoma, Oklahoma City, Oklahoma, July 18, 1979.

John A. Lander, President, Girard College, Philadelphia, Pennsylvania, October 30, 1979.

Mrs. Gordon (Phyllis) Maybee, RR 1, Debert, Nova Scotia, June 25, 1980 and October 20, 1981.

Jeanette Prather, Smith Funeral Home, Anadarko, Oklahoma, May 14, 1981.

A. A. Padilla, Records Control Supervisor, U.S. Penitentiary, Leavenworth, Kansas, June 17, 1981.

Phillip J. Roberts, Research Historian, Wyoming State Archives Museums, and Historical Department, Cheyenne, Wyoming, March 28, 1979 and November 21, 1978.

Mrs. Bess Sheller, County Librarian, Carbon County Public Library, Rawlins, Wyoming, November 5, 1979.

Ferris E. Stovel, Judicial and Fiscal Branch, Civil Archives Division, National Archives and Records Service, Washington, D.C., February 1, 1979.

Mrs. Carl (Jessie) Sundstrom, Custer Chronicle, Custer, South Dakota, June 24, 1980.

Jean Thebrand, Deputy Consul, Consulate General de France, New York, New York, June 27, 1979.

Dave Walter, Reference Librarian, Montana Historical Society, Helena, Montana, February 20, 1979.

Billy D. Ware, Director of Classification and Records, Texas Department of Corrections, Huntsville, Texas, July 17, 1979.

Russell H. White, Sheriff, Woodbury (Iowa) Sheriff's Department, Sioux City, Iowa, February 18, 1982.

D. L. Wilbourne, Manager, Records Department, U.S. Penitentiary, Leavenworth, Kansas, May 8, 1979, May 25, 1979 and May 27, 1981.

Mrs. Ida Wozny, Archivist/Historian, Wyoming State Archives, Museums, and Historical Department, January 25, 1979.

Related Correspondence

W. H. H. Llewellyn, Special Agent, Department of Justice, Deadwood, Dakota, to Hon. Charles Devens, Attorney General, Washington, D.C., September 15, 1880, Record Group 60, National Archives and Records Service, Washington, D.C.

INDEX